POPULAR MECHANICS

QUICK HOME
IMPROVEMENT

POPULAR MECHANICS

QUICK HOME
IMPROVEMENT
TIPS

BY THE EDITORS OF *POPULAR MECHANICS*

Steven Willson
Home Improvement Editor

Gary Branson
Contributing Writer

Illustrations by
George Retseck and Don Mannes

HEARST BOOKS
New York

It is the policy of William Morrow and Company, Inc., and its imprints and
affiliates, recognizing the importance of preserving what has been written,
to print the books we publish on acid-free paper, and we exert our best
efforts to that end.

Library of Congress Cataloging-in-Publication Data
Popular mechanics 101 quick home improvement tips / edited by Steven
Willson ; foreword by Joe Oldham.—1st ed.
    p.   cm.
    ISBN 0-688-11754-6
    1. Dwellings—Maintenance and repair—Amateurs' manuals.
I. Willson, Steven.   II. Popular mechanics magazine.   III. Title:
Popular Mechanics one hundred and one quick home improvement tips.
IV. Title: Popular Mechanics one hundred one quick home improvement
tips.
TH4817.3.P63   1992
643'.7—dc20   92-7200
                                                                                              CIP

Printed in the United States of America

First Edition

1 2 3 4 5 6 7 8 9 10

BOOK DESIGN BY MICHAEL MENDELSOHN OF M 'N O PRODUCTION SERVICES, INC.

CONTENTS

FOREWORD

Popular Mechanics has always provided its readers with in-depth advice and know-how on home improvement. With this handy volume, we've gathered together solutions to some of the smaller and more perplexing problems that emerge in the course of owning a home or renting an apartment. Although the pace of modern life is hectic, *Popular Mechanics 101 Quick Home Improvement Tips* is for everyone who enjoys the feeling of accomplishment that goes along with the time spent preserving the creature comforts and value of a home.

Through simple step-by-step illustrations, we offer mastery—at your fingertips—of the most persistent repair and maintenance tasks that you as a homeowner or renter may encounter. Whether it's replacing a broken door handle, reenameling a chipped bathtub, quieting a squeaky floor, unsticking a stuck window, or patching a hole in a carpet, user-friendly help is at hand. If your sights are set on your lawn and garden, you can learn how to revive a worn lawn, compost trash, or paint a wooden fence. An extensive glossary will help you speak the language of professionals, and a section on basic tools will help you select the right materials when it comes time to visit a hardware store. You'll even find tips on electricity, heating and cooling, and plumbing so you can head off problems before they occur, and a special section on safety tells you how to dispose of hazardous wastes and household products.

Our aim, as always, is to provide you with the best advice and ideas for improving your home. You'll find that *Popular Mechanics 101 Quick Home Improvement Tips* is filled with both.

Joe Oldham
Editor-in-Chief
Popular Mechanics

CHAPTER ONE

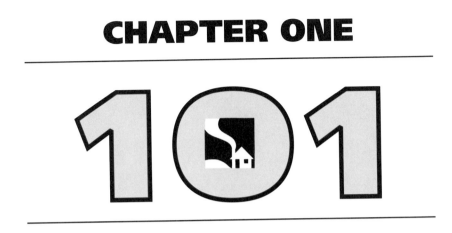

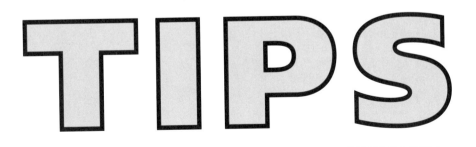

Ladder Safety

Many home repair chores require the use of a ladder, so we should learn to handle ladders safely. According to the U.S. Consumer Products Safety Commission, 97,000 people were treated at hospitals for injuries resulting from ladder use in 1989. These injuries could be avoided by choosing and using a ladder in the proper way.

First, read and heed the labels on ladders. Ladders are rated for their intended use and the load they will bear. Keep in mind that the load or *duty* rating of a ladder refers to the *total* weight it can carry, not to the worker's weight alone. This limit should include the weight of the heaviest person in your household, plus the weight of any tools and materials carried up the ladder.

Ladders are rated by type. Type I can hold 250 pounds, Type II holds 225 pounds, and Type III will hold 200 pounds. If you are over 200 pounds, buy a Type I or even the Type IA, which will support 300 pounds. This will allow a safety margin if you ever climb a ladder with a bundle of roof shingles.

After reading the ladder's label for weight limits, check any warnings printed on the ladder. The top of a stepladder is not a step, nor is the tool tray that is commonly attached to fold out at the back of the ladder. In

Read and heed all label warnings printed on any stepladder, particularly the caution against using the tray shelf as a step.

Periodically check the step brace nuts to make sure they are tight. If not, securely tighten each with an adjustable wrench.

addition to observing warnings, you should be aware that ladders are most stable when your weight is kept centered between the ladder legs. Leaning or reaching can cause the ladder to topple. If you can't reach far enough, climb down and move the ladder.

Ladders are commonly made of wood, fiberglass, or aluminum. Aluminum extension ladders have become popular because they are lightweight and easy to move. But one common accident occurs when aluminum ladders hit overhead power lines, or when homeowners use electric tools while working on the ladders. The metal conducts electricity, making it a potential hazard. So, watch where you move your ladder, avoid hitting power lines, and buy cordless tools to help prevent electrical shock.

2 Heeding Label Warnings

If you ask paint dealers what is the best advice they can give consumers, they will always reply: "Tell them to read the labels." Most of us think we know how to apply the paint or use the chemical in the container, so we neglect the instruction side of the label. But do you understand what terms such as "flammable," "use with adequate ventilation," and "keep away from heat and flame" really mean? Knowing how to work with chemicals can save your health or your life.

Paints or other chemicals that can be fire hazards are listed as combustible (least flammable), flammable, or extremely flammable. Remember that the fumes of flammable chemicals are also flammable. In fact, fumes such as gasoline are a greater threat for fire or explosion than liquid gasoline. Avoid using any flammable product near any appliance that has a pilot light. Remember, too, that fumes are heavier than air and settle toward the floor, where low pilot lights can ignite them. The best rule is to use flammable chemicals outdoors.

What does the phrase "use with adequate ventilation" really mean? Many people think that if they open a window, ventilation needs are met. In fact, the warning means that ventilation should be such that fume dispersal is equal to what you would have if working outdoors. The fumes from some of these chemicals can damage you or your home. Paint removers especially have been a risk. So never use them indoors without shutting off the furnace and opening windows and doors. You can augment air movement with a fan set in a door or window to pull outside air in.

Finally, the warning "keep away from heat and flame" means just that: The chemical and its fumes are flammable, and represent a hazard of fire or explosion. This warning, of course, implies a ban on smoking or any other activity that requires an open flame.

Childproof Your Home

Burns, falls, electrical shock, and drowning are all hazards for children. Here are some tips to follow so your child won't become a statistic.

- Did you know that, according to the Consumer Products Safety Commission (CPSC), 125 infants have drowned since 1985 in 5-gallon pails left unattended by their parents? It's true. An infant can climb headfirst into such a pail. Keep children away when you are using any large open containers for washing cars, windows, or other chores.

- Buy extension cords that have protective plug covers. These covers should be in place whenever any slots are not being used. Open slots in that socket can provide the opportunity for infants to stick metal or other objects into the holes. Also buy inexpensive outlet covers that plug into unused outlet openings. And don't let appliance cords hang from countertops. Use twist wires to fold and tie the cords so an inquisitive child cannot grab the cord and pull down a hot appliance.

- Turn handles of cooking pots inward so children cannot grab pot handles and dump boiling contents.

If you use extension cords around young children, be sure to use cords that have protective covers for the unused outlets.

Even the apparently harmless 5-gallon pail is a risk for young children. They could drink poisonous contents, or climb in and drown.

- Turn down your water heater thermostat so a child cannot be scalded accidentally in the bathtub. Adults may know to mix in cold water if the faucet runs too hot, but children may turn the hot faucet on while they are in the tub, with disastrous effects.

- Check all container labels and place dangerous chemicals or anything with a poison label in a locked cabinet. And don't leave caustic cleaning products under the sink cabinet to be discovered by a young child.

Three-Prong Installation

Homes of the fifties or older may have 2-slot electrical receptacles, which means that the entire electrical system was grounded through the cable that connected the outlets. The cable, a flexible steel tube called *greenfield*, tied the entire system together, rather than using a third wire as today's Romex cable does.

These old outlets are safe, but often inconvenient. You must use a grounding adapter plug to connect any tool or appliance that has a 3-prong grounding plug. A better idea is to simply replace old 2-slot receptacles with 3-slot models, especially in frequently used outlets.

The first step is to turn off the electrical current to the circuit at your fuse box or breaker panel and use a neon tester to be sure no current is present. Remove the outlet cover, then pull the old receptacle out of the box and loosen the wire screws on both sides.

When you have disconnected the old receptacle, attach the wires to the new receptacle in the same way. Then attach a pigtail ground wire (available at hardware stores and electrical supply houses) to the green screw at the bottom of the new receptacle. The pigtail has a spring clip that must be pushed over the edge of the metal outlet box. Replace the retaining screws that hold the receptacle to the box, add the cover, and turn on the power.

Adapters should not be kept on electrical cords as shown. They should be attached to the outlet with the covering plate screw.

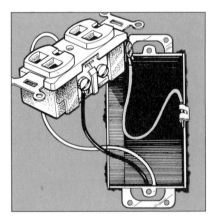

Wire a 3-pronged receptacle just like a 2-pronged one. But add a grounding pigtail and clip from the receptacle to the box.

Correct Bulb Sizes

On lamps or ceiling light fixtures, you may see a warning to use 60-watt bulbs only or some similar restriction. The reason for this warning is the chance of heat buildup and fire if you use a hotter, oversized bulb in the fixture. Recessed and flush-mounted light fixtures are especially at risk from heat buildup and fire because there is no air circulation around the fixture to cool the bulb.

For example, the flush-mounted fixture shown in this drawing has a cover that traps the heat from the bulb. Additionally, the bulb itself lies flat against the metal base, which in turn is attached directly to ceiling tile. The heat buildup in such a fixture can lead to a fire even if the bulb you are using is only 15 watts higher than the recommended size. If you need more light, either add another fixture or replace the existing one with something that can use a more powerful bulb.

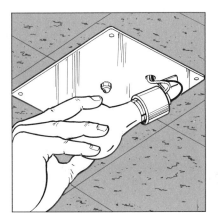

Ceiling light fixtures that provide little clearance around the bulb will easily overheat if improper high-wattage bulbs are used.

Installing Smoke Alarms

If you haven't provided your home with fire-protection alarms, by all means do so. When strategically placed, these alarms can provide the few seconds of advance warning needed for your family to escape injury or death from fire or smoke. Keep in mind that most house fires occur at night when your family is sleeping and most in need of a warning.

You should install smoke alarms on every floor of the house. Fires most often occur in kitchens, furnace or appliance rooms, and attached garages. Install an alarm at the top of each staircase, near heating equipment in the basement, and in the hall outside bedrooms.

The alarms are not expensive, and battery-powered versions are easily installed. The only tool you'll need is a screwdriver. New alarms will not only sound if smoke is detected, but a light will also go on to help the family find its way to safety. Such alarms cost around $18, even less on sale. Test your alarms frequently to make sure the batteries are fully charged.

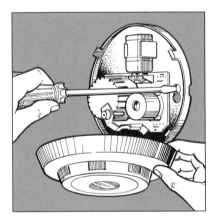

Smoke alarms are so easy to install that there's no reason for not having several in every house. You only need a screwdriver.

Preserving Polarity

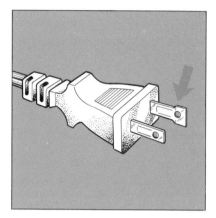

The wire blade on an electrical plug (arrow) maintains circuit polarity. Because of it, the plug can only be inserted one way.

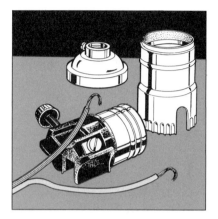

Light-duty wire insulation is smooth on one side, ribbed on the other. To maintain polarity, attach ribbed wire to silver screw.

Perhaps you have read instructions for doing electrical repairs that warned you to connect the white (neutral) wire to the silver terminal, and the black (hot) wire to the brass terminal. This color-coding technique ensures that you will not cross wires and create a dangerous short. In addition, only black (hot) wires should be switched in your house. Of course, you could turn off the light if you switched the white (neutral) wire, but the light socket would still be hot. And you would run the risk of getting shocked if you directly handled the light socket, even though the light switch was off.

To ensure this continuity or polarity, lamps and small appliance cords have a wide blade on one side of a cord plug and a narrow blade on the other side. The wide blade only fits into the wide slot in a polarized outlet. Because of this, you cannot turn the plug over and make the neutral wire the switched wire. Even the simplest and least expensive lamps are wired so that the switched wire is the black or hot wire, and therefore no electric current is flowing into the socket when the switch is turned off.

When you replace the cordset on a lamp, be sure to check the wire you are using. One side of the replacement wire should have a ribbed finish, while the other side will be smooth. If both sides are smooth, don't use the wire. Always wire the lamp with the ribbed side connected to the wide-blade side of any plug, and the smooth wire connected to the narrow-blade side of the plug. When you attach the wire to the new (or old) lamp socket, be sure the ribbed wire is connected to the silver screw, and the smooth wire is connected to the brass screw. By doing this, the black (hot) wire will always be the switch wire.

Here's one more tip for rewiring a lamp. If you want a custom-looking job, instead of buying a separate wire and plug, buy a 6-foot-long extension cord that already has a molded plug attached. Cut off the outlet end of the cord and strip off the insulation to attach the wires to the lamp socket. This is a good idea because the extension cord is cheaper than buying the wire and plug separately, and you have a much nicer, molded plug.

8 Hazardous Wastes

Homeowners are constantly being bombarded with warnings of hazardous wastes. What are the guidelines for determining which household materials are hazardous?

Most states now classify as hazardous any waste product that meets these criteria:

- Any ignitable liquid or gas, or any solid that could easily ignite at ordinary temperatures or pressures.

- Any waste that contributes oxygen or other reactive gas to a fire.

- Any material that is highly caustic or acidic.

- Any material or chemical that reacts violently or produces dangerous fumes when in contact with water.

- Any material that may give off toxic chemicals when dissolved in a landfill or other acidic environment.

- Any chemical that is toxic to animals or persons when inhaled, drunk, eaten, or in contact with the skin.

A list of household wastes that may be potentially hazardous if improperly used or handled include: most wood preservatives, pesticides, herbicides, fertilizers, paints, varnishes, paint thinners, and cleaning solvents.

To reduce common yard and garden products in the waste stream: 1. Strictly observe the application instructions on any container; 2. Use all of the product before discarding the container; 3. Shop for products that are environmentally safe.

Many paint solvents and thinners are made unnecessary by the new water-based paints and finishes that are available today. For example, modern chemical combinations have made acrylic latex paints nonfading and easy to apply. The acrylic latexes are so tough they are now used as a wear surface on concrete floors.

CHAPTER TWO

101

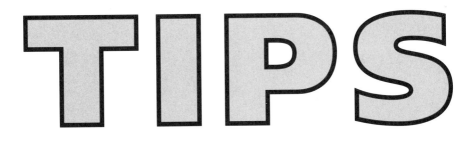

PLUMBING

TIPS

9 Flush Lever Replacement

Whether your toilet flush lever breaks, or you just want to change it to match other hardware, lever replacement is a simple, 10-minute chore. Begin by removing the top of the toilet tank and unhooking the chain or strap that connects the lever to the tank flapper below. Inside, you will find a retaining nut on the back side of the lever. Hold the lever on the outside of the tank with one hand, then, using adjustable pliers, remove the retaining nut from inside the tank. Do not inadvertently tighten the nut—or drop tools on the tank—because the tank could crack.

To install a new flush lever, insert the arm of the lever through the hole in the toilet tank. Install and tighten the retaining nut, then connect the flapper strap or chain to the lever. Flush to test.

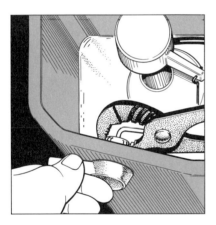

To replace a toilet flush lever, first remove the tank cover and find the retaining nut. Remove the nut with adjustable pliers.

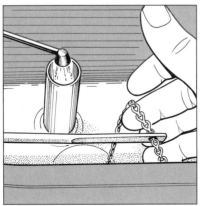

Slide the new lever into the tank hole and tighten it in place with its retaining nut. Then hook the flapper chain on the lever.

Preventing Drain Clogs

Knowing how to unclog blocked drains is very useful, but preventing the drains from becoming plugged in the first place is the better idea. Most drain blockage occurs because of materials that never should have reached the drain. Homeowners often cause themselves embarrassment and expense by pouring leftover patch materials and paint down drains, where the materials solidify and cause clogs. Let these materials harden, then dispose of them in the trash.

Another good idea is to install a filter on your washing machine drain hose to trap fibers and lint before they can go into the drain. One of the best filters is the foot from a pair of discarded pantyhose. Its finer weave will catch smaller particles than stock filters will. And keep in mind that the primary causes of bathtub drain clogs are soap particles and human hair, so it's a good idea to discard soap bars before they disintegrate into clog-size particles.

Finally, when operating your kitchen disposer, be sure to run plenty of water down the drain while the disposer is on. And continue to run the water for a minute or two after the disposer is off. This ensures that all the ground garbage has reached your main drainpipe, not just your smaller sink wasteline.

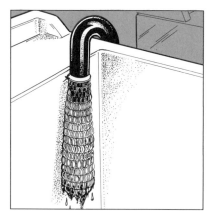

One way to minimize drain debris is to install a filter, made of stocking material, on the end of your washer's drain hose.

11 Cleaning Fiberglass Tubs

A common problem in newer homes is how to clean tubs, shower enclosures, or laundry sinks made of fiberglass. Molded fiberglass products were an instant hit with homeowners because of their joint-free construction and lack of periodic maintenance. But owners soon found that soap or mineral films clung to fiberglass and were difficult to remove.

If you have a fiberglass product that is dull and/or stained, avoid using abrasive cleansers or cleaning pads. They can scratch fiberglass finishes, making them very difficult to repair. Instead, use a quality fiberglass cleaner, usually available at supermarkets and hardware stores.

Once clean, you can make the fiberglass easier to reclean and more stain resistant with an application of automotive-type paste wax. Bear in mind, however, that the floors of a shower or bathtub may become slippery if waxed. Consider using wax only on surfaces you do not walk or stand on.

If mineral buildup is very heavy, you should do something about your water quality. Water treatment experts can install filters in water lines to remove the staining minerals. Installing a water softener can also reduce staining, especially if soap scum is the problem, because soft water will leave less soap residue.

Finally, when you've dried yourself after a bath or shower, take time to wipe down the shower or tub with your bath towel.

Never use abrasive cleaners on any fiberglass fixture because they will scratch the surface. Instead, use fiberglass cleaners.

Bathtub Refinishing

Replacing a bathtub can be a messy and expensive job. That's one reason why more folks are turning to bathtub refinishing. However, depending on the color of the tub and where you live, a professional epoxy resurfacing job can cost between $200 and $250. On the other hand, do-it-yourself refinishing kits cost about $75. While these kits can be made to work, many people report a high failure rate. The problem lies in getting a good bond between the new epoxy coating and the old tub finish.

To get the best bond, you must get the bathtub as clean as possible. The pros do the job by giving the tub a strong bath with industrial-strength acid. You can, however, get fairly good results by using a very strong solution of TSP (trisodium phosphate), available at paint dealers and home centers. Follow the directions for mixing an extra-strength solution, or as recommended for removing paint. Wear eye protection and rubber gloves when using this solution.

Clean the tub with the TSP solution and a scrub brush or sponge. Scrub the tub repeatedly—this is the most important step of the job. If you fail to get the surface clean, the epoxy will peel off. After washing the tub thoroughly, rinse it with clear water.

The next step is to wet-sand the surface with 80-grit wet/dry paper. Again, this must be a complete job—or the new finish may not adhere. The final step is to apply the epoxy. This comes in a resurfacing kit that contains the necessary tools—rollers and brushes—plus the epoxy finish and instructions.

Because professionals use heat to cure their epoxy finishes, they estimate that the new surface will last for up to seven years. With careful cleaning and sanding, a homeowner should get at least five years from a refinished tub before the process has to be repeated.

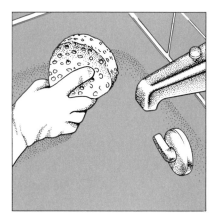

Wash the tub thoroughly with a sponge or brush, using a strong solution of TSP. After several washings, rinse the tub.

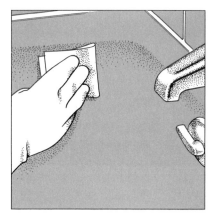

After rinsing, roughen the surface by sanding with 80-grit wet/dry paper to remove the glaze from the porcelain.

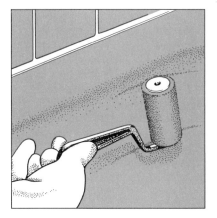

Mix the epoxy finish according to manufacturer's instructions. Use a brush and rollers supplied in the kit to apply epoxy.

13 Fixing Bathtub Stoppers

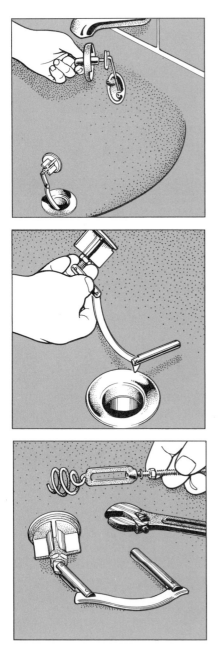

To gain access to the bathtub stopper assembly, remove the two screws that hold the overflow plate. In this Standard brand bathtub, the stopper rod is connected to the plate.

When you have removed the overflow plate and lift assembly, you can lift the stopper assembly and rocker arm out of the drain for cleaning or replacement.

There are two adjustment points on the stopper. The first is a nut just under the stopper on the top end of the rocker arm. The second adjustment can be made by turning a small nut above the spring on the assembly. Adjust these nuts as necessary to make the stopper open and close completely.

Modern bathtub stoppers may have built-in pop-up features: If you step on the stopper it seals the drain; step again and the drain plug pops up. But older bathtub stoppers may have a stopper that is activated by a lift assembly rod connected to a lever that is mounted on the tub overflow plate.

Because the bathtub stopper and components are exposed to a hostile environment of water, soap scum, and corrosion, you should take the assembly apart periodically to clean and lubricate it. If neglected, the lever assembly may become corroded so it cannot be operated. The stopper should be wiped clean of soap residue and hair.

Bathtub stopper assemblies vary according to the manufacturer and they are not interchangeable. If the lever seizes, you can buy replacement parts for most bathtub stopper assemblies, but because of the difference in the assemblies you may be unable to find replacement parts at your home center. In this case, you must seek out a plumbing dealer who handles parts for your particular bathtub. Check the Yellow Pages of your phone book to find a dealer for a particular manufacturer: For example, the unit shown here is a Standard brand model so you must replace parts with that brand.

Vacation Checklist

If you spend time away from home on business or take extended family vacations, you may be overlooking simple steps that can protect your home and save you money. Remember, strange things can happen when a house is left unattended. In one case, remodeling homeowners decided to take a three-day weekend break from their fix-up tasks. In the process of remodeling a bathroom the couple had removed the old plaster and bathtub. However, they did not turn off the water to the bath. In their absence, an invading squirrel climbed onto the water faucet to reach a bag of peanuts left on the vanity. In its scramble to climb the squirrel turned on the faucet and the homeowners found the house flooded on their return. Make a vacation checklist of things to do to secure your home while you're away and try to anticipate any potential problems.

- If you'll be away in cold weather remember that you should keep the home temperature above freezing to protect the plumbing and prevent cracking of plaster and concrete basement walls. But you need not hold the furnace thermostat above a minimum 60 degrees: higher temperatures are necessary only for human comfort. Set your furnace thermostat on the lowest setting (usually 60 degrees) to save energy costs.

- No need to maintain hot water at normal temperatures when no one's home. Turn the water heater thermostat to low, or turn off the heater completely to save energy while you are away. This way, you will also avoid a burst water heater if it fails while you are away.

- If you have an older house where burst plumbing pipes are a possibility, shut off the water supply at the gate valve near the water meter. This step could save a possible flooding and water damage to your home.

- No matter the age or condition of your plumbing, you should shut off the water supply faucets to your automatic clothes washer before leaving home. Better yet, shut off the hot and cold water supply to the machine after each use. If you leave the water faucets on full-time, you are using the washer hoses as though they were water pipes: obviously, washer hoses can break and flood the laundry. So turn off water supply faucets after each washing, and replace the washer hoses every three to five years if you leave the washer running when you go out.

To save energy and money turn down the thermostat on the furnace and the water heater before leaving for vacation.

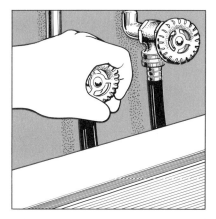

Shut off water supply faucets to washing machine before leaving home. Burst washer hoses can flood the laundry area or basement. If plumbing is the old galvanized water pipe, shut off water supply at the main valve near the water meter.

Stopping
Water Hammer

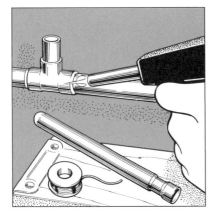

Solder a ½-inch T into the water supply pipe as near as possible to the faucet.

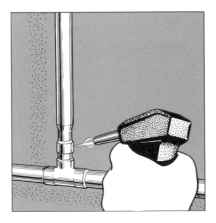

Be sure the T fitting is positioned at the top. Solder the air chamber into the T.

In modern city water systems the water pressure may reach 90 pounds or so. When water is run at a faucet the water is moving under this high pressure and velocity, so if the faucet is turned off abruptly, the water may stop with a bang that may even be audible. This stop is especially abrupt at an automatic washing machine, where the shutting of a solenoid valve can produce a loud bang. The common term for this phenomenon is "water hammer." Water hammer not only makes an annoying noise but it also can vibrate water pipes and loosen or crack fittings and joints.

The cure for water hammer is to install an air chamber, sometimes called a shock absorber, at the end of the pipe run, as close as possible to the faucet or washer where the water hammer is occurring. The air chamber may be a simple closed copper tube or it may be a plastic ball that contains an enclosed rubber bladder. In either type of air chamber, the water column is pushed against trapped air. Unlike water, air can be compressed. The water in the pipe compresses the air and cushions the shock, stopping the water hammer.

To install the copper air chamber, cut out a section of the water supply pipe and solder a "T" fitting in the line. The copper air chamber must be installed so the top is up to prevent all air from being driven from the chamber. Solder the air chamber in place to complete the installation. If your project will not permit installation of a vertical air chamber, you can install a plastic model instead. The plastic water hammer arrester, such as one made by Genova, contains a rubber bladder inside the arrester. Air is trapped inside the arrester, between the plastic bulb and the bladder. In this model the air cannot be pushed out and the arrester can be installed in any position—even upside down or horizontal.

Replacing a Bathtub (Diverter) Spout

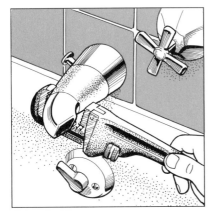

Wrap masking tape around the spout to improve the grip of the wrench jaws and to avoid damaging the spout finish.

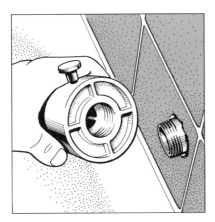

Buy a replacement spout that has a plastic sleeve and threads. The plastic threads will not rust or corrode, making future removal easier.

In many bathtub/shower plumbing arrangements the waterspout has a diverter valve. If one wants to fill the tub, the diverter valve is pushed down and water flows into the bathtub. If one wants to take a shower, the diverter valve is pulled upward. This shuts a valve in the spout so that water is forced to flow upward into the shower head. Over time the diverter valve may become fouled by mineral buildup or corrosion. When this happens the diverter valve may only partially close, so that a portion of the water flow runs into the tub, and a portion of the water is diverted into the shower head. This can result in an unsatisfactory water volume running through the shower head. To correct this condition, the defective diverter spout must be removed and replaced with a new spout. To replace the spout, you must have a pipe wrench or large pliers with adjustable jaws. To avoid damaging the finish on the spout, wrap the spout with a thick layer of masking tape before turning the spout with the wrench or pliers. If the spout has been in place for many years, the threads on the spout and the water pipe may be corroded, so the spout may be difficult to remove. Be sure the jaws of the wrench or pliers have a firm grip on the spout, and apply pressure on the tool carefully to avoid having the tool slip and damage the tub or tile.

When the defective spout is removed, use a wire brush or steel wool to clean the threads on the water pipe. Apply a thin film of plumber's grease to the pipe threads to ease installation of the new spout. New diverter spouts have a molded and threaded plastic sleeve inside the metal spout. The plastic sleeve makes installation easier, and also will ensure no rust or corrosion on the spout threads, making future spout replacement much easier.

17 Sink Trap Replacement

Hidden away under most plumbing fixtures you will find a U- or J-shaped pipe called a trap. The trap serves several functions. The most important function of a plumbing trap is that it traps and retains water in the lower bend, thus blocking the drain so that odors and sewer gases cannot flow back into the house. The trap also provides a first line of defense against plugs by catching any materials that might form a plug farther down the drain where it would be more difficult to remove. Traps are also easy to remove for access to the piping if a drain plug does occur.

Considering that metal drain traps are constantly full of water, and thus constantly exposed to rust and corrosion, one might wonder how they last as long as they do. Today, plastic traps are available that may last literally forever, but in time the metal traps will fail and need replacing. The only tool you'll need to replace a trap is a pipe wrench or a pair of adjustable-jaw pliers. Most metal and plastic traps are interchangeable but you'll find it's usually easier to replace a metal trap with metal or a plastic trap with plastic.

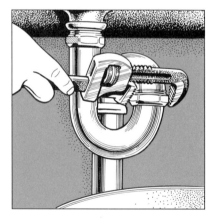

Place a small pail under the sink trap to catch any water spills. Use a pipe wrench or adjustable pliers to remove the old trap.

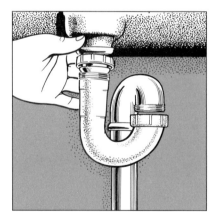

Wrap Teflon plumber's tape around the pipe threads and install the new trap. Turn on the water and let it run while you check under the sink for leaks.

Replacing Washing Machine Hose Valves

18

In the laundry room you will find a pair of washer hose valves (faucets) that control the water supply to the automatic washing machine. These faucets are provided so that the water to the washing machine can be shut off for repair or replacement of the machine. Also, because the washing machine is connected to the water supply via a pair of short rubber hoses, the water supply faucets should be shut off when the washing machine is not in use. If you leave the faucets open so there is constant water pressure on the rubber hoses, the hoses may break and flood the laundry area. For this reason you should shut off the faucets when the wash cycle is finished. If you often let the washing machine run while you are away, replace the water hoses every three to five years, to ensure that the hoses can contain the water pressure without rupturing.

Over time the faucets will develop leaks, either through the faucet spout or around the stem. Because the hot water will deteriorate the stem washer faster than cold water will, the hot water faucet usually will begin to leak first. However, because you have to turn off the water supply at the meter to repair the faucets, it is best to repair both hot and cold water supply faucets while you have the water off and the tools and washers handy. The washer's hose faucets can be taken apart for repairs by turning the nut on the top of the faucet. Use a pipe wrench or adjustable pliers to loosen the nut. With the nut unthreaded you can pull out the stem of the faucet.

On the bottom end of the faucet stem you will find a washer, secured to the stem by a single small screw. Because faucet washer sizes vary by faucet type and manufacturer, it is best to buy a package of assorted washer sizes to be sure you have the right size washer on hand for repairs. Remove the screw and replace the washer with one of the same size. Reassemble the faucet and turn the water on to test for leaks.

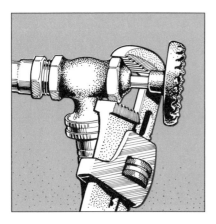

Turn off water supply at the main valve near the water meter. Open faucets to purge water from faucets. Use a pipe wrench to unscrew the top nut from the washer and remove the faucet stem.

Use a small slot screwdriver to remove the washer screw. Lift out the worn washer and replace it with a new washer of like size.

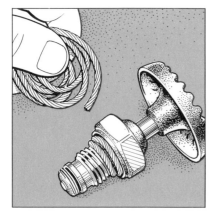

Some faucets have a packing nut at the top and you must wrap twist packing around the stem to stop water from leaking upward past the stem. Wrap one round of twist packing around the stem under the packing nut.

19 Water Heater Maintenance

Water heaters can survive heavy duty service, usually without a whimper. The first sign you may see of water heater failure may be no hot water, or water running out under the heater, sure signs that the heater needs attention or replacement. But a few simple steps can extend the heater life and keep it operating properly.

If you have water that is hard or has a high mineral content, attach a garden hose to the drain valve or place a plastic pail under the drain valve near the bottom of your water heater. Turn on the water and let it run until it is clear and free from any sediment. Minerals or deposits that form in a layer at the bottom of your water heater can insulate the water from the burner's heat below, extending recovery time for the water heater and wasting fuel.

You will also see a water tube and a small valve on the side of the water heater. This is the pressure relief valve, designed to prevent dangerous steam buildup if the heater malfunctions. Place a catch pail under the end of the water pipe and lift up on the relief valve to be sure the valve is still operable.

When the (gas-fired) heater burner is on, light a match and hold it under the hood on the exhaust vent at the top of the water heater. If the

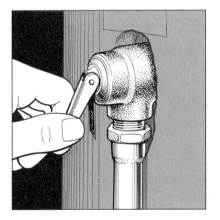

Place a pail under the pressure relief valve pipe and lift the relief valve to be sure this safety device is still operable.

vent is open, the flame from the match should flicker upward. The hood and vent pipe are held in place by one or two small sheet-metal screws into the larger furnace duct pipe. If your heater is several years old, remove the vent pipe, clean it, and reinstall it in place. Remember to set your heater thermostat low enough so that no one will be burned or scalded by hot water from the heater.

 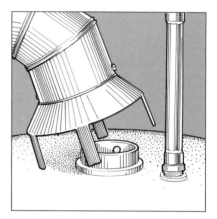

When a gas water heater is in the burn cycle, hold a match or lighter under the vent pipe hood atop the heater. If the vent is open, the flame will flicker upward.

Remove two small sheet-metal screws to lift the water heater vent pipe free and clean out the vent pipe.

20 Cleaning a Kitchen Sink Sprayer

Shower heads and sink spray heads can become clogged and corroded with time. The primary problem is mineral content in the water—lime, calcium, or iron. So, the most important step for keeping plumbing fixtures working is water quality. If your house has its own water well, or city water contains a high mineral content, you may want not only to soften the water but to install filters in your main line to improve the water quality.

Be sure water is turned off. Disconnect the spray head from the hose and disassemble the spray head by removing the screw cover and screw inside the head tip. Soak the sprayer head parts in vinegar or a lime cleaner, rinse, and reassemble.

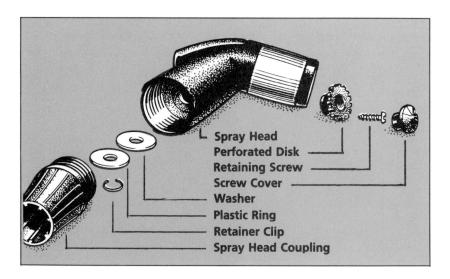

Spray Head
Perforated Disk
Retaining Screw
Screw Cover
Washer
Plastic Ring
Retainer Clip
Spray Head Coupling

If the sink sprayer head does become plugged, it's an easy task to clean it. Turn off the water supply to the sprayer head. Disconnect the sprayer head from the hose, laying out any parts in the order that they are removed. Then use a small screwdriver to pry off the screw cover in the spray nozzle. Remove the small screw inside the nozzle to get access to the seat and perforated disk inside the sprayer head. Use a toothbrush to clean the parts of the sprayer head. Stubborn minerals such as lime will often yield to a soak bath of ordinary vinegar. For tougher cleaning jobs buy a lime cleaner chemical at your home center or plumbing supplier. Some of these lime cleaners contain phosphoric acid and may damage such materials as polished aluminum or ceramic tile. Read and follow all label warnings.

21 Renewing Tub and Tile Caulk

Ceramic tile can be a very durable material if properly maintained. But if grout and tub/tile caulk are neglected, water may penetrate to the tile base or substrate, damaging either the tile adhesive or base and causing the tile to loosen and the entire tile job to fail.

Check the ceramic tile often for signs of cracks in the grout or tub/tile caulk. You no longer have to mix a messy powder grout: premixed latex grouts are available and easy to apply. But because grouts become brittle when they set, you should not use ceramic tile grout to seal the crack between the bathtub and the ceramic tile. A brittle grout at the tub/tile crack would quickly crack again. Instead, choose either a latex tub/tile caulk in a squeeze tube (no caulking gun needed) or a preformed, peel-and-stick tub/tile caulk strip.

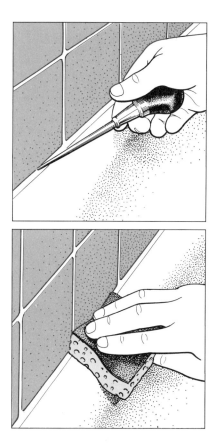

Use a sharp carpenter's awl or an ice pick to remove the old caulk from the joint between the tub and tiles.

Thoroughly clean the joint area with ordinary rubbing alcohol to remove the soap scum.

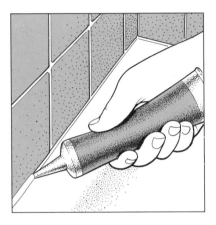

Fill the tub and tile joint with a latex caulk, available in a squeeze tube. Tool the caulk joint with a wet finger or a Popsicle stick.

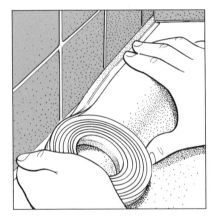

An excellent option to using paste caulk is to buy a preformed caulk strip. To apply the caulk strip just cut it to length and peel away the adhesive strip on the back. Press the caulk strip into the corner, forming a neat and decorative trim joint.

CHAPTER THREE

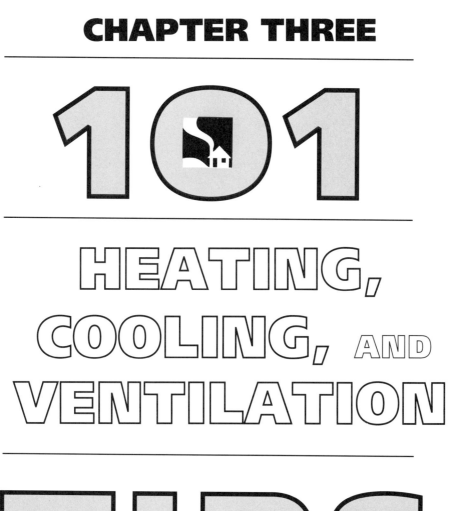

101

HEATING,
COOLING, AND
VENTILATION

TIPS

22 Bathroom Moisture

A common homeowner complaint is moisture buildup, often with mildew, in the bathroom. The procedures to eliminate the problem include finding and reducing the source of the moisture, making sure that proper ventilation is present in your bathroom, and changing personal bathing habits in order to minimize moisture.

The first step is to find out where the moisture is coming from. Check your plumbing to be sure there are no leaks in the pipes under floors or in walls. If you find leaks, high humidity can be the least of your problems: Damaged wall tile, loose floor covering, or rotted floor joists are all possibilities. Repair all plumbing leaks.

If you see water seeping around the base of the toilet, it means that the wax ring needs replacing. The wax ring seals the joint between the toilet and the waste drainpipe.

Moisture may be due to sweating of the toilet tank which is caused by cold water that cools the tank and, in turn, causes the humidity in the room to condense on the tank and run onto the floor or wall. To stop condensation, buy a terry-cloth tank cover to absorb the moisture. Better still, have a plumber install a mixing valve that warms the water coming into the toilet tank.

If excess moisture is due to steam from bathing, shaving, and other activities, install an exhaust fan to remove the moist air from the room. Or keep the bathroom door open so the humidity can circulate outside and mix with drier air in other rooms. You can also wipe down the shower or tile with your bath towel when you have finished drying yourself. And don't leave wet towels in the bath. If necessary, use a small bath fan to circulate the moist air and reduce moisture levels and mildew growth.

 Ventilation Checkup

Good ventilation is necessary to prevent winter ice dams on your roof and other moisture problems in any season. Though you may have had your ventilation and insulation updated for energy savings, it's a good idea to check the attic and roof each spring to make sure everything is working.

The best ventilation is continuous soffit ventilation for the length of the house combined with full continuous ridge venting. This setup creates a natural chimney effect that pulls cool air in at the soffits, moves it across the insulation blanket where it picks up moisture and heat, and then exhausts it out at the ridge vent.

Climb into the attic to check the insulation. High winds can blow fiberglass about, even though wind velocity is reduced by the soffit vents. Check also to make sure that no insulation is blocking the airflow where the roof truss or rafter crosses over the top plate of the outside wall. Clear away any obstructions so the air can flow freely between the soffit and ridge vents. Also check the underside of the roof deck for water stains, which may indicate a roof leak or the buildup of frost and moisture in the attic during winter. Any sign of moisture in the attic indicates either a roof leak or insufficient roof ventilation.

Inspect rooftop ventilators once a year to make sure they're still securely attached to the roof. Check inside by removing turbine.

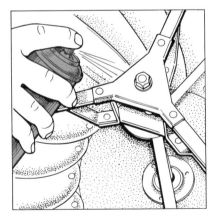

Wiggle the turbine shaft to check for bearing wear. Then lubricate the bearings using a spray lubricant. Reattach the turbine.

Next, go on the roof and check any rooftop ventilation. If you have a turbine vent, check the turbine for wear by wiggling it from side to side. Any excess play on the shaft indicates bearing wear and early failure of the turbine. To make the turbine last longer, remove it from its base and lubricate its bearings using an aerosol penetrant and lubricant, such as WD-40. Reassemble the turbine and check for smooth operation.

24 Stopping Air Leaks

To reduce air infiltration, caulk between the sill and foundation, and install batt insulation between the joists above the sill.

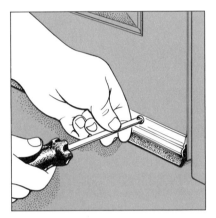

Inspect all door sweeps for fit. If they are loose, tighten them. But if worn, replace them with new layered vinyl versions.

One vital key to reducing home utility bills is to block air leaks with insulation, weather stripping, and caulk. Whether the air is *conditioned* for winter heating or summer cooling, it is essential that we do not let this air escape to the outside. Contractors and energy inspectors tell us that two of the most commonly overlooked cracks in the house are where the sill meets the basement wall and under exterior doors where the door meets the threshold.

The crack between sill and basement wall is the longest continuous crack in the house because it includes the total circumference of the first floor. Check the crack to see how large it is. If this crack is very large, you can fill it with plumber's oakum or twisted strands of fiberglass insulation, followed with caulk until the crack is filled completely. Once the crack is filled, cut fiberglass insulation batts to fit in the space where floor joists and sill meet.

Advances in door weather stripping include door sweeps, made of vinyl, that often have multiple, overlapping layers to ensure a seal between the bottom of the door and the threshold. Inspect the door sweep on all exterior doors and install the best sweep you can find at replacement time.

25 Furnace Maintenance

If your home has a forced-air furnace, the blower unit does some pretty heavy work moving all the heated air. And if the furnace incorporates central air conditioning, your blower unit may run at high speed almost all year long. Because of this, read your owner's manual and apply lubrication to the blower motor as indicated. (Some furnace blower units are sealed and permanently lubricated, so check the manual to see which kind you have.)

On our forced-air furnace, the blower motor is secured by two sheet-metal screws. We removed these retaining screws and pulled the blower unit forward to reach the oil ports on the motor shaft. Then we applied a couple of drops of 30-weight oil to each oil port. It's a good idea to do this oiling at least twice a year. But if your owner's manual suggests more frequent service, follow the recommendation.

Both furnace servicemen and interior decorators will tell you that most people neglect the furnace filter. The filter is an inexpensive but important component of good furnace operation. The filter removes dust and dirt from the air as it enters the main return duct at the bottom of the furnace. All the air is filtered to preclean it before it enters the furnace, which helps keep the furnace clean. Neglected filters will lose their effectiveness, letting dirt pass through. Under these conditions, the blower unit on your furnace becomes little more than a dirt-circulating machine.

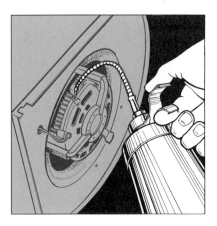

Consult your owner's manual for the oil port locations on the furnace. Then remove the blower cover and apply oil to the ports.

45

26 Central Air Maintenance

Modern central air conditioners require little attention from the homeowner. The most common maintenance step is to replace the filter in your furnace monthly during peak air-conditioning season. This will ensure a free flow of clean, cool air. But the air-conditioning equipment will also benefit from extra attention.

Check the top of your compressor for screw locations. By removing a few retaining screws, you should be able to easily lift off the top. When you have access to the fan motor, check your owner's manual for lubrication and cleaning needs. It should reveal the lubrication ports on the motor that need oil. Use an oiler with a flexible tube to place a few drops of 30W motor oil in each oil port. Usually these ports are at one or both ends of the motor shaft. Be sure to replace any plastic caps that cover the ports to prevent dirt or water entry.

Use a garden hose with a spray nozzle to clean the finned tubing inside the housing. The fins help dissipate heat from the copper piping. Because outside air is drawn in over these pipes or coils, they can become coated with dust. (You may be amazed at the amount of grime you will rinse out of those coils.) Remember, the unit has to work harder to remove heat

To maintain an air conditioner, remove the cover, then wash away any dirt from the coils using a garden hose and nozzle.

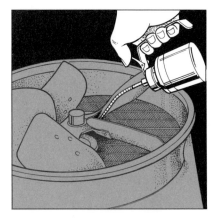

Consult your owner's manual to determine proper lubrication points for the fan motor. Then add oil as required and replace cover.

if the coils are layered with dirt. Flush out all the dirt before you replace the cabinet top and screws.

Finally, a compressor that sits in direct sunlight will work harder to dissipate heat. If your yard compressor is in direct sunlight, especially if it is on the west side so it receives the sun's hottest afternoon rays, consider building a shade screen around the compressor. One option is a lattice-and-ivy screen that will not only protect the compressor, but look great, too.

27 Super Air Filters

The inexpensive filter in the cold air return of your forced air furnace is called a dust-stop filter. As air moves, it picks up all sorts of pollutants, so the dust-stop filter is used to filter out large dust, lint, grease, or pollen particles. These dust-stop filters primarily keep the furnace ducts and blower unit clean: They will not filter out smoke, most pollens, viral matter, mildew spores, or smaller dust particles. An estimated 99 percent of indoor air pollutants are microscopic in size and cannot be trapped by cheap dust-stop filters. If you suffer from allergies or bronchial ailments, you should consider upgrading your furnace filter.

While dust-stop filters will trap particles that are 100 microns or larger in diameter, superior media air filters screen out larger particles and trap smaller particles on fibers inside the filters. Media air filters can filter out particles as small as 0.5 microns, a great improvement over ordinary dust-stop filters. Media air filters can be purchased from your heating supply dealer or hardware store for $8 to $10 each.

To keep the forced air furnace blower and duct work clean, along with your home's interior, change dust-stop filters monthly. For those with allergies or bronchial conditions, consider installing a superior media air filter or an electronic air filter for the best protection.

The best air filters are electronic filters that can trap particles as small as .01 micron, meaning they can remove such small particles as pollen, plant and mildew spores, dust, smoke, bacteria, and some viruses. Ask your heating contractor for information on these electronic filters. Some electronic filters can cost upward of $1,000 (professionally installed), but keep in mind that if your physician orders such measures for a member of your family you may be able to deduct the electronic filter as a medical expense. Also, new thinner electronic air cleaners are being developed by the Emerson Electric Co. (9797 Reavis Rd., St. Louis, Mo. 63123) that fit easily into the furnace cold air duct and can be installed by the homeowner.

28 Tuning Furnace Ducts

Are you an empty nester with unused rooms because your children are away at college or on their own? Are your heating bills too high? Are some rooms in your house too warm and others too cold? It's time to tune the heating ducts on your forced-air furnace.

When your house or replacement furnace was new, the heating mechanic adjusted or "tuned" the dampers in your air ducts. Because the mechanic was unaware of your life-style or living patterns, the best he could do was to try to see that conditioned air was distributed somewhat evenly to all rooms in the house. Rather than readjust the duct dampers to their own needs, most people have lived with the damper adjustments that the heating mechanic chose, and used the wall or floor-mounted air registers to control the flow of warm air in winter and cool air in summer.

If you are unhappy with the air supply distribution in your house, you can tune the duct dampers to suit your own living style. For example, if you have extra bedrooms that are seldom used, you may want to shut the duct dampers to those rooms.

Many people close the wall air registers, thinking they can save energy and money by not heating or cooling a room or rooms. The problem is, if you force the conditioned air down that duct, you have already paid to condition it but you are not using it. Rather than shutting the wall registers, shut the damper in those ducts to unused rooms, so that the conditioned air is not delivered where it is not needed, and fully open the duct dampers to rooms where conditioned air is needed. For example, shut duct dampers to unused bedrooms or guest rooms. Rooms that are close to the furnace are being served up the hottest air: shut dampers to those rooms and open fully duct dampers that serve the rooms most distant from the furnace.

The first step is to locate all air ducts and to be sure which duct serves which room or area. The furnace air ducts in most homes are accessible from the basement or crawl space. Check the ducts to find the dampers, and check to see whether they are open or shut. On the duct dampers shown, there is a locking nut that must be loosened in order to adjust the dampers. The shafts on the dampers have screwdriver slots in their bases: turn the dampers with a slot screwdriver to adjust them, then tighten the locking nuts to hold the dampers firmly in place.

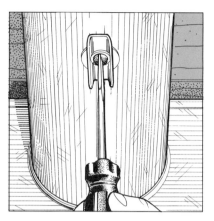

Locate the dampers on all the various furnace air ducts. The duct dampers in this house have locking nuts that can be loosened by hand.

When the locking nuts are loosened, use a slot screwdriver to turn the damper open or shut. After turning the duct dampers, observe the way the house heats or cools. Further turning may be necessary for family comfort.

29 Hot Water Radiators

Hot water radiator heating has been around for many decades, and for good reason. Hot water heat is an even, draft-free and economical means of warming a house. In older systems the hot water heating system consists of a water boiler where a burner heats the water, piping to deliver the hot water to radiators and to return the cooled water to the boiler for reheating, and heavy cast-iron radiators that absorb the heat from the water and radiate it into the house. This type of hot water heating might be a gravity-style unit, or might have a slow circulating pump. Newer hot water systems consist of a water boiler, a delivery system of copper piping, with aluminum fins on the copper pipe to disperse the heat at small baseboard radiators. Because these copper pipe and aluminum fin radiators have little ability to absorb and radiate the heat from the water, high-speed pumps are used to move the water swiftly through the copper piping.

Whatever type of hot water heat you have, your most common maintenance chore will be to check the radiators for trapped air. Air trapped in the radiator chambers prevents water from flowing into the chambers. If you have cold radiators in some rooms, you must loosen the screw of the bleeder valve to let or "bleed" the air out of the chamber. Simply turn the bleeder valve until you hear a sputtering or hissing noise. That noise is the air escaping from the chambers. Leave the bleeder valve open until only hot water runs out, without hissing or bubbling. A steady stream of water indicates that all the air is out of the radiator. Close the bleeder valve and check the radiator to be sure it warms up properly.

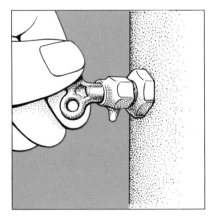

To release any trapped air in a hot-water radiator, open the brass bleeder valve with a hexhead key or screwdriver.

30 Maintaining Steam Radiators

If you have a radiant steam heat system most problems may be solved by replacing one of two components. One component that can fail is the steam vent, found at the top corner of the outside cell of the radiator. The second component that may cause problems is the steam-trap bellows, found at the bottom corner of the radiator where the radiator outlet pipe and condensate pipe meet.

The steam vent is a cone-shaped device at the top of the radiator. Over time the vent may become clogged with minerals. Although you may be able to clean away some of the mineral residue to open the steam vent, the best long-term cure is to replace the steam vent. Turn off the inlet valve to the radiator, then turn out the steam vent. In most cases you will be able to unscrew the steam vent by hand. Then coat the threads of the new steam vent with anti-seize compound to make installation and future removal easier. If a steam radiator heats poorly and emits a pounding noise, the problem is with the steam-trap bellows. As steam cools and condenses in the radiator, the steam trap collects the water and directs it back to the condensate tank. The bellows in the trap is heat sensitive and opens to let cold water return to the condensate tank, but snaps shut to trap the hotter steam in the radiator. When the bellows fails and does not shut, the steam can escape from the radiator along with the condensate, producing a pounding noise and causing the radiator to fail to heat properly.

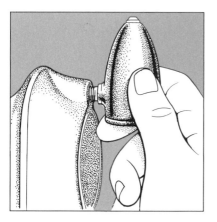

To remove a clogged steam vent, first turn off radiator inlet valve to isolate radiator. Then, simply unscrew vent.

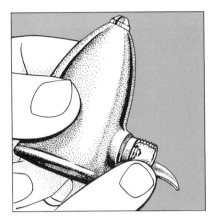

Before installing new steam vent, coat the threads with antiseize compound. Then tighten by hand until snug.

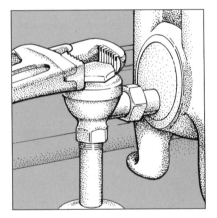

Use a pipe wrench to loosen steam trap cap and gain access to trap bellows. If necessary, tap with hammer to loosen threads.

The thermal bellows is flexible, allowing it to expand and contract. Replace bellows even if no defect is visible.

To remove the old thermal bellows, use a pair of pliers or small wrench to unthread it from the steam trap cap.

After threading the new bellows into the cap, coat the cap threads with compound and tighten the cap in place.

Use a 12-inch pipe wrench to remove the cap from the steam trap. Use adjustable pliers to unscrew the bellows from the cap. Because the replacement bellows may not look just like the old bellows it is best to take the old bellows along to the heating supply dealer to be sure to get a compatible replacement bellows. To ease installation and future removal, coat the threads on both the thermal bellows and on the steam-trap cap with antiseize compound.

31 Seal Air Leaks Around Electrical Outlets

If you've taken all the obvious insulating and weather stripping steps to reduce heating and air conditioning costs, any future energy conservation will be possible only with attention to little things—for example, sealing the little cracks that can permit air infiltration and can add up to big losses of conditioned air. The rule for stopping air infiltration is to seal up any crack you can find. If the crack is between two materials that do not move, caulk them tight. If the crack is between a nonmoving material (such as a door or window frame) and a moving component (such as a door or a window), install weather stripping. But sealing small cracks, such as those around electrical outlets, can also pay big dividends on heating and cooling bills.

To stop air infiltration around an electrical outlet, first turn off power to the outlet to avoid electrical shock. Then remove the outlet cover. If there are cracks between the plaster or wallboard and the outlet box, fill the cracks with spackle or taping compound. Use a putty knife or your fingertip to fill and smooth the crack. Let any patch material dry, then fit foam plastic insulation covers over the receptacle or switch. Install these insulation covers at all electrical outlets that are on outside walls to stop air infiltration and conserve energy.

Unscrew electrical outlets and then use spackle to fill cracks between the wallboard or plaster and the electrical outlet box. Install the foam insulation over the electrical device.

CHAPTER FOUR

101

DOORS AND WINDOWS

TIPS

32 Garage Door Weather Stripping

The weather stripping at the bottom of your garage door provides a seal against water, cold air, dust, and insects. If this strip becomes torn or worn, it's easy to replace it because the strip is only attached with galvanized roofing nails. Just pry off the old strip and nail on a new one. Check with your door manufacturer for instructions on steel or fiberglass doors.

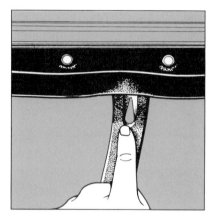

If your garage door weather stripping is broken or torn, it should be replaced. Remove the old one by prying it off with a flat bar.

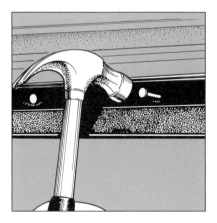

Cut the new weather stripping to length, and then nail it to the bottom edge of the door using galvanized roofing nails.

33 Garage Door Tips

Keeping your home in shape through preventive maintenance is the best method for keeping those big, expensive jobs at bay. One area that benefits from periodic attention is your overhead garage door. With a quick inspection and a little cleaning and lubricating, you can keep your garage door working properly day after day—plus extend the life of the door's hardware and components.

The first step in maintenance is to check the hardware. Tracks, brackets, and rollers can loosen under the load of constant use. Tighten any loose screws or nuts on the door hardware.

Next, clean the door track regularly to avoid a buildup of dirt and oil. The residue that develops when dirt and oil combine can cause the door to bind, which can eventually damage other components or the door itself. Use a cloth or sponge soaked in a solvent such as mineral spirits to scrub the track until it's clean.

The final step is to lubricate every piece of hardware that moves, such as locks, tracks, and hinges. If you have a garage door opener, lubricate the mechanism that raises and lowers the door. Also check that the components are adjusted properly according to the manufacturer's specifications.

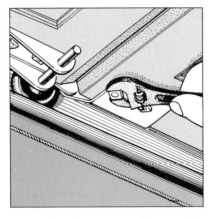

Inspect hardware to make sure it's secure and in good condition. Tighten any component that's loose.

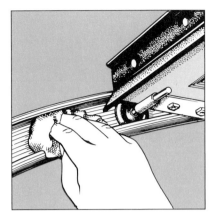 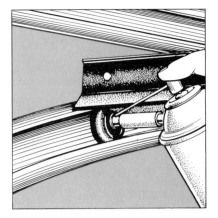

Use a clean cloth or sponge soaked in a solvent such as mineral spirits to wipe away all dirt and grime from the door track.

Lubricate all moving parts. Use a convenient aerosol spray lubricant to reach track rollers, locks and door hinges.

34 Shortening Hollow-Core Doors

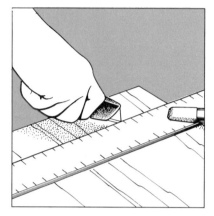

Clamp a straightedge to the door at the cutoff line. Then use a sharp utility knife to cut through the veneer.

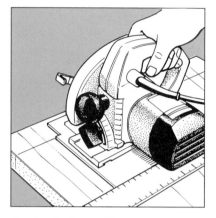

Cut to the line with a sharp circular saw. Clamp a straightedge in place to accurately guide the saw along the scored line.

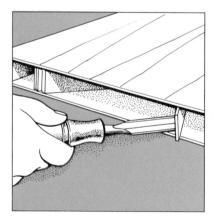

If you've cut into the door's hollow core, use a chisel to remove or push back the braces from inside the door cavity.

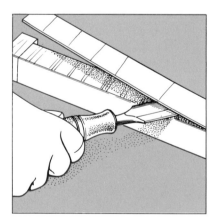

Use a sharp wood chisel to remove the veneer from both sides of the end-frame member. Scrape off all the old glue.

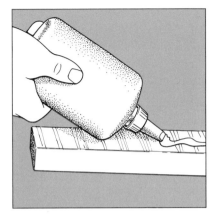

After the veneer has been removed and the end-frame member is cut to length, apply carpenter's glue to both sides.

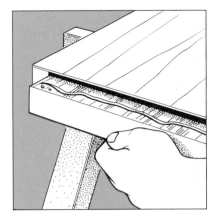

Insert the frame piece into the door cavity. Align it flush with door end, clamp until glue dries, and remove excess glue.

If you ever try to shorten a hollow-core door, you may find yourself with a job you didn't bargain for. Because hollow-core doors have a hollow, honeycombed interior, cutting off more than one or two inches can completely remove the structural member at one end. Not only does this leave the open core exposed, but the structural integrity of the door is affected.

To do the job, first mark the end to be cut. If you're trimming the door to suit a raised floor or new carpeting this will always be the bottom. Then remove the door by driving out the hinge pins with a screwdriver and hammer. Place the door flat on a pair of sawhorses.

Use a straightedge to mark the cutline on the door. Then clamp the straightedge to the door and cut along the line with a sharp utility knife. Cut completely through the veneer to help prevent the veneer from splintering when you make the cut. Use a square to carry the line to the opposite face, and score the veneer on this side as well. Using a sharp blade in your circular saw, cut just to the outside of the scored line. It's best to use a straightedge to guide your saw precisely along the line, and adjust the blade so it just protrudes through the opposite face of the door.

If you've cut into the hollow core of the door, you must replace the end frame member that you've cut away. First, reach into the open end of the door and push back or cut away the cardboard braces that you'll find. Then use a sharp chisel to strip the veneer from the frame on the waste piece. Apply carpenter's glue to both sides of the frame. Gently pry apart the veneers on the door, and insert the frame into the hollow core.

Align the edge of the frame so it's flush with the veneer face edges. If you're customizing an existing door that's already painted or varnished, wipe away the excess glue with a damp cloth. If it's an unfinished door, wait until the glue begins to set, and then peel it away with a sharp chisel. Clamp until the glue dries. Use at least three clamps with wooden strips placed between the clamps and the door to evenly distribute the pressure. After the glue has dried, remove the clamps and ease all sharp corners by light sanding with 120-grit sandpaper.

35 Maintaining Storm Doors

Maintenance on metal storm doors with their sliding windows and screens is often neglected—until things stop working properly. If you're having trouble opening and closing windows or screens, it's time to clean and lubricate the unit.

The first step is to check the sashes to be sure they're in the proper channels. If the retaining pegs at the sash top are in one channel, and the latch mechanism is in another channel, the window will bind if you try to slide it up. If it's not aligned, push in the latch buttons and withdraw the window from the channel. Then reinstall the window so it's aligned in one track.

To clean and lubricate the unit, remove the window and screen frames. Use a paintbrush or sponge paint applicator and mineral spirits to clean dirt and grit from the channels. Soak a clean cloth in mineral spirits and wipe the edge of the window and screen frames. Lubricate channels and sash edges with spray lubricant.

After you've cleaned all the channels, windows, and screens, reinstall the components in the door frame. Make sure that the sashes are properly aligned and in the correct channels. Then check that the windows and screens move freely.

To remove a sash, push the latch buttons on both sides of the frame inward. Pull out bottom and disengage top pegs.

To remove dirt in door frame, dip a brush or sponge paint applicator in mineral spirits, and clean the channels.

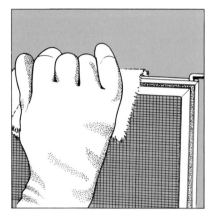

Wipe the frames of the windows and screens with a cloth soaked in mineral spirits to remove dirt and grime.

Lubricate the frames, latches, and sash channels with a spray lubricant. Then reinstall the sashes, and check operation.

36 Adding Door Hinges

Using a sharp chisel, cut a mortise within the lines to accept one hinge leaf. The depth of the mortise should match the leaf thickness.

To add a third hinge to any door, just buy one that matches the size and shape of the existing hinges and trace it on the door.

Because they are made of solid wood (or metal) and are heavy, exterior entry doors are usually hung on three hinges. Interior doors, on the other hand, are lightweight and usually have only two hinges. The 2-hinge system is sufficient for most interior doors, but if you decide to add weight to the door, you may have to install an extra hinge to help support the added weight. Over-door clothes hangers and door-mounted mirrors are additions that can greatly increase the weight on the door. And you must either reinforce the door with an extra hinge or face the possibility that the door will sag under the weight.

To add an extra door hinge, first remove any added weight. Then use a screwdriver and hammer to drive up the hinge pins and remove them. With the door removed, lay it across a pair of sawhorses or, preferably, stand the door on edge with the hinge side up. To help hold the door upright, push one end of it into a corner of the room.

Next, using a hinge that matches the existing ones, mark the hinge outline on the door edge, midway between the other two hinges. When you have marked its outline, use a chisel or a router to cut a mortise (recess) for the hinge. You must also mark and cut a hinge mortise on the door frame. Once these cuts have been made, screw the door side of the hinge to the door, and the frame side of the hinge to the door frame. Reinstall the door. The added hinge support will now hold any reasonable weight you place upon it.

37 Storm-Door Handles

If you break the door handle on your aluminum storm door, don't consider replacing the door. These days, you can buy replacements for anything—including storm-door handles. The only thing you will need to know is the spacing between the retaining screws that hold the interior and exterior parts of the lock together. Remove the old lock handle and measure the distance between these screws, or take the old lock and handle assembly with you when you go shopping for a replacement.

The replacement lock kit will contain the new lock and handle, plus retaining screws and extra shims for moving out the old strike plate, if necessary. Replacement couldn't be easier. Just remove the screws from the old lock unit, position the new unit, and secure with the new screws. You may have to loosen the two screws of the strike plate and add the shims in order to make sure the storm door latches securely.

To get the proper replacement handle for your storm door, remove the old handle and take it to the store to get a perfect match.

Sticking Windows

There are few things more frustrating than a window that will not open. Unfortunately, most of us pay no attention to our windows until they start to stick. But a little periodic maintenance is all it takes to keep them running smoothly.

First of all, clean the window channels with a hand vacuum or a tapered nozzle on your floor vacuum. Next, apply a lubricant to the channels. Keep in mind that some vinyl channels in modern windows should not be lubricated, but older windows with metal channels require lubrication to keep windows moving smoothly.

In truth, most balky windows are caused by sloppy paint jobs. A too-full brush will let paint drip and run between the sash and stop, painting the window shut. When painting, remember to use the minimum paint and to move the window up and down several times during the drying process.

If all this advice is too late, and the window is already stuck or sticking, do not try to force the sash. You may damage the window, break the glass, or injure yourself. Instead, pick up a serrated tool, usually called a *window zipper*, at your local hardware store. The tool has a blade shaped like an arrowhead, so it will fit into almost any crack. And the edge of

To free a window that's painted shut, slide a paint-cutting tool between the sash and stop. Then pull the tool around the sash.

When repainting the window, use the minimum amount of paint, and move the sash up and down frequently while the paint dries.

the blade is notched or serrated like a bread-cutting knife. This notched edge will cut through just about any paint in the cracks. But for stubborn cases, you may have to pry loose or unscrew the stop strips that hold the window in the sash. When you have removed the stop, sand or scrape the edges of both stops and sash to remove excess paint. Then repaint both edges and let them dry before you reinstall the stops and sash.

39 Painting Window Sashes

When you paint windows you should let the paint overlap slightly onto the glass to ensure that you have a moisture seal between the window sash and the glass. If you try to mask window glass to protect it from paint, you will find that the masking tape may cover the slim crack between the glass and sash, and the open crack will fill with moisture when the window sweats (on the inside) or when it rains (on the outside). When water or moisture penetrates into the sash, the window will begin to rot. So don't mask glass.

Instead, buy a quality paintbrush designed for painting the line between glass and sash. A good brush will have thick bristles that hold together when wet with paint, instead of spreading apart and covering adjoining glass with paint. Most pros prefer a tapered sash brush or a 1½-inch-wide trim brush for cutting around window glass.

If you have never used a professional-quality brush, you will be amazed at the difference it can make. Poor-quality brushes will lose bristles as you paint, leave brush marks from the cheap, coarse bristles, and spread as you brush, making it almost impossible to paint a straight line.

Another secret is to *wipe* the paint line when you are done. Wrap a piece of clean cloth over the tip of a paint scraper or putty knife and wipe away excess paint from the glass. Periodically, move the cloth so the part covering the tool blade is clean. And keep from dragging the remainder of the cloth over surrounding painted surfaces. When done properly, this technique should yield a straight and clean paint line.

To ensure a straight paint line on glass, wrap the end of a putty knife with a clean rag and pull the knife across the surface of the glass.

40 Sticking Locks

Most houses have only two or three exterior door locks, and removing, cleaning, and lubricating each takes only a few minutes. All the tools and materials required are the right screwdriver—slot tip for older locks, Phillips-head tip for newer locks—and an aerosol lubricant/penetrant such as WD-40.

There are four screws holding a door lock in place. Two retaining screws hold the interior and exterior parts of the lock together, and two more screws hold the faceplate of the latchbolt to the door.

Remove all four screws and pull the handles apart, then slip the latchbolt out of its hole. Spray the moving parts of lock assembly liberally, flushing out all dirt and old lubricant. Products such as WD-40 combine penetrant and lubricant properties, so they can be used both to clean and to lubricate at the same time. Do not use grease for a lubricant. It becomes stiff in cold weather and will make the lock difficult to operate. Grease also will hold any dirt or grit that gets into the lock. Sticking locks on interior doors can be fixed in much the same way.

A final tip: Periodically clean your keys to remove dirt and lint from the grooves because the lint picked up from your pockets can plug locks. Once clean, be sure to spray your keys with WD-40 and let them dry. The lubricant will help keep the keys clean and fit easily in the locks.

To repair a sticking lockset, first remove it and thoroughly clean all the parts. Then spray them with lubricant and reinstall.

Removing Paint

Paint buildup from repeated coatings can cause cracking or alligatoring. Older plywood surfaces such as the panels on garage doors are especially susceptible to such cracking of paint. Any additional painting will only make matters worse. You must remove all the old paint and start over to eliminate the problem.

To strip the old garage door shown, we used 3M's Safest Stripper—the first of the growing number of water-based paint removers. These strippers have a gel consistency, so they won't run and drip when applied to vertical surfaces. And, generally speaking, they don't have high evaporative rates, which means they can be left on the surface for hours without requiring a reapplication. Of course, the best part of these new strippers is that they aren't toxic. The fumes are safe and barely detectable, and contact with the skin poses no problem.

New, nontoxic paint strippers are easy to use and have long open times. You can work for hours before the stripper dries out.

42 Replacing a Window Screen

Warm weather means it's time to throw open your windows, but it's also time to repair broken window screens. Start by buying a 2-wheeled spline roller, vinyl spline, and screen at a hardware store.

Now, pry the vinyl spline and damaged screen from the frame groove using an awl or a sharp knife tip. Discard the old spline; in most cases it is too dry and brittle to reuse (besides, new spline is inexpensive). Use a razor knife to cut a piece of screen slightly larger than the frame, then lay the frame on a table and the screen over it. Tape each edge of the screen to the table, and make a diagonal relief cut at the screen's corners, stopping at the frame groove. The relief cut prevents the screen from tearing at the corners or bunching up when it is rolled into the corner of the frame.

Press the screen into the frame groove on one side with the convex roller. This will cause the tape to pull loose from the table. Pull the screen tight from the opposite side and repeat the process. Do this on the other two sides. Press the spline into the groove with the concave wheel. Trim off excess spline and screen with a razor knife.

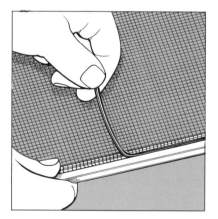

Lift up the old vinyl spline using an awl or other sharp tool, then peel it out of the frame. Next, remove the screen.

After slitting screen corners, place new screen over frame, and tape it down. Roll screen into frame with convex wheel.

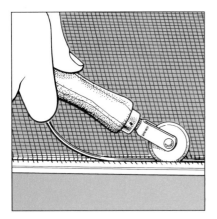

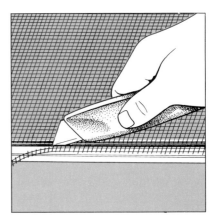

Cut new vinyl spline roughly to length. Then roll it into the frame with concave roller at opposite end of the spline tool.

Trim off the excess screen using a razor knife. Press the knife's tip into the outside edge of the spline groove.

CHAPTER FIVE

101

YOUR HOME'S EXTERIOR

TIPS

43 Moss Problems on Wood Roofs

Moss and mildew love a moist climate, so moss or mildew growing on your wood roof indicates that your roof is not draining well after a rain. Sources of roof moisture can be a lack of sunlight to dry the roof deck (usually caused by trees or adjoining buildings that shade your roof) or the result of leaves, twigs, or other debris that collect on the roof and hold moisture. Additionally, the spaces between shakes or shingles are meant to aid water runoff. Leaves and other debris that block these paths also block good drainage and prevent proper runoff.

The first step to a dry, moss-free wood roof is to cut away any branches that overhang the roof and block out sunlight. Exceptionally thick limb growth on trees should be remedied by a professional tree trimmer who can selectively thin the branches so that sunlight can filter down to the roof deck. This thinning of treetops can also open the space to better ventilation, and proper ventilation or airflow across the roof aids the drying process.

The next step is to inspect the roof for debris that may be trapped in valleys, behind chimneys, or in the cracks between the shakes or shingles. Vegetable debris, such as leaves, acts like a sponge on the roof surface, soaking and holding moisture in the cracks or gaps between shingles. This

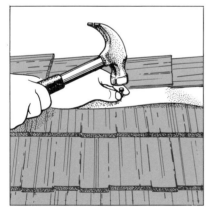

Adding a strip of zinc near the ridge of a wood roof inhibits the growth of moss. Install the strip with galvanized nails.

can be alleviated by trimming back tree limbs, but it may be necessary to power-wash the roof once or twice a year to keep it clean and free of debris.

A product commonly used in the far West is a strip of metal that is 97 percent pure zinc. The zinc strip is nailed at the edge of the ridge or below the level of anything that blocks water flow, such as vents or chimneys. As rainwater washes down the roof, it picks up zinc from the strip, and the zinc inhibits future moss growth.

One such product is named Z-STOP and manufactured by WESPAC (P.O. Box 46337, Seattle, WA 98146). To use Z-STOP, first power-wash or brush away the existing moss. (For severe cases, you can buy a herbicide from your local garden center that will kill moss.) Then use roofing nails with neoprene washers to nail the Z-STOP in place along ridges, gables, or skylights.

44 Maintaining Rain Gutters

Rain gutters that become clogged or drop water in the wrong location can cause soil erosion and basement water problems. Tour the exterior of your house to check how your roof gutter system is working, and whether water is directed away from the foundation, driveway, patio, and other things that could be undercut by erosion. Water that pours along a blacktop or concrete driveway, for example, can erode the soil, wash away and undercut the gravel base from underneath, and leave the top unsupported so that the weight of an automobile could break it.

Check your rain gutters at least twice a year, in the spring and in the fall, to make sure that they are clean and securely attached to the house. Check downspouts to be sure they have not been loosened by roof ice or snow loads. Next, check the ground pipes to be sure water that reaches the ground is carried away from the house's foundation. Of course, splashblocks, placed under the ground pipes or downspouts, help direct water away from the house.

If water coming from ground pipes or downspouts is causing a problem, you may have to redirect the pipes so that the water flows out in a better direction. Sometimes this means moving the downspout to a different location and changing the pitch of the rain gutters. But more frequently, all that's required is rerouting or lengthening your ground pipes. Generally speaking, a ground pipe should carry water at least 8 feet away from the house's foundation.

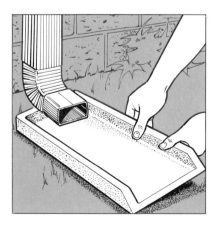

Use splashblocks under downspouts to direct water away from house. This reduces the chance of water entering your basement.

45 Repairing Rain Gutters

Gutters can get beat up over the winter from ice and storm damage. Here are a few tips to get them back in shape for the summer rains ahead.

Variable-speed electric drills are great for gutter work because you can set them at low speeds. High drill speeds are fine for woodwork, but a fast-turning bit will spin on a gutter downspout or gutter bracket without cutting.

Mark where you want to drill with a metal punch. The dent left by the punch holds the bit while it bites into the metal.

Use pop rivets to join gutter components together. Usually only one or two rivets are necessary to hold pieces together. To remove a rivet, just drill out its head with a ⅛-inch-diameter bit. Run the drill slowly until you have drilled through the rivet head. Remove the head and punch out the rivet shank with the metal punch. Seal all repairs to the gutter with silicone or other suitable caulk, but this isn't necessary on downspouts.

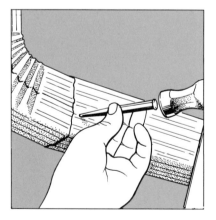

Use a metal punch to make a small dent over where you want to drill. Dent holds drill bit as it bites into metal.

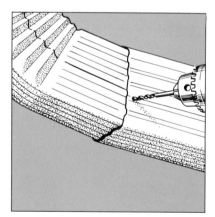

Run the drill at slow speed and don't force the cut. High-speed, high-pressure drilling can overheat the bit, dulling it.

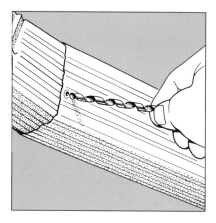

Use a slightly oversize bit to smooth burrs around the rivet hole. Lightly turn the bit with your bare fingers.

Fasten parts together with one or two aluminum rivets. On downspouts, top part always goes inside part below it.

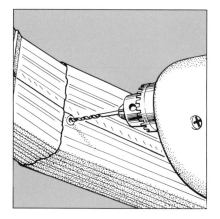

To remove a rivet, drill through its head with a bit matching the rivet's diameter, usually ⅛ inch diameter.

46 Cleaning Rain Gutters

If there are lots of deciduous trees near your house, you'll need to clean your rain gutters at least twice a year—after the seeds blow in spring and after leaves drop in fall. Gutters that are clogged with leaves or debris can cause water backup that runs under shingles or overflows the gutter rim, and washes down to stain the siding or windows below. Keep your gutters clean so the system delivers roof water to downspouts, then away from the house foundation to ensure a dry basement.

Cleaning gutters is not a hard job, assuming the gutters are within easy ladder reach of the ground. If gutters are two stories or more above-ground, you might consider hiring a roofer for this sometimes dangerous task.

While you're climbing to clean rain gutters, conduct your spring roof inspection. Check for windblown shingles, beginning rust on valleys or vents, and check flashing where fireplace chimneys or walls intersect the roofline.

Use a power washer or garden hose and spray nozzle to flush debris from the gutters. Check the debris as you flush it away. One early indica-

If your house is surrounded by trees, wash out all your gutters at least twice a year to remove debris like leaves, seeds, and twigs.

tion of roof failure is to find a lot of granules from the asphalt shingles washed into rain gutters.

As you flush the debris from the gutters, check the water flow. Are there low spots in the gutters where water can pool? If so, raise the gutter at this point and rehang it so it empties properly. Also, watch the water flow from the downspout at ground level. If the water flows swiftly away from the foundation, you'll have a dry basement. If the water flows toward the house or gathers in puddles near the basement, you may have basement moisture problems in the making. Correct the ground pipe direction so water flows away from the house.

 Painting Roof Vents

Today's new houses usually have prepainted aluminum vents and flanges, but on older houses, the choice was often galvanized steel. Galvanized metal does resist rusting. But it's best to give it a coat of paint periodically to prevent rust that will, in time, permanently stain your roof shingles.

The first step is to clean it with mineral spirits. Then apply a coat of metal primer, followed by a topcoat of metal paint. The paint not only will protect the metal from rust and corrosion, it will also help vents, valleys, and flashing to blend in with the roof shingle colors. Note that we recommend that you use *metal paint* only for painting metal components. House paint is much too thick for use on metal. And a too-thick paint film will blister and peel—a condition that's all too common on gutters and downspouts painted with house paint.

If the fixture has already been painted, but is peeling, use sandpaper or a wire brush to remove loose paint. If rust is present, apply a coat of rusty-metal primer first.

If metal vents or flanges need painting, first brush off the old flaking paint and then mask the surrounding roof with paper and tape.

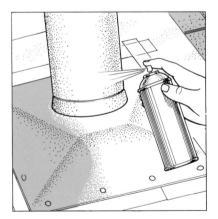

Spray a metal primer on the surface first. Then let it dry and spray on one or two top coats. Keep the coats thin to prevent runs.

48 Patching Masonry Cracks

In the past, one of the most difficult and frustrating home repairs was trying to patch cracks in masonry products like concrete and stucco. Most cracks are due to expansion and contraction of the masonry when temperatures change. So the movement that caused the crack almost invariably caused the patch to fail. In addition, masonry products are not adhesive, so they don't stick well to the old surface. Because of this, the old advice was to begin by chiseling out an inverted V in any crack. This was supposed to create a mechanical bond between the old and new materials because the patch material would be locked in place by the joint configuration. The failure rate of such patches proves the system was lacking.

Today, patch materials, usually with an acrylic latex base, are available in caulk tubes. These repair caulks are adhesive, so they will stick to almost any clean surface. This allows you to successfully patch concrete slabs, steps, retaining walls, and stucco. Patching cracks in brick joints, however, is a bit more of a problem, because the patching products may not match the color of the existing mortar joint.

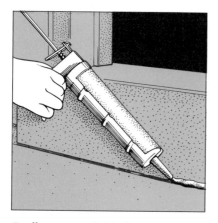

Caulks are available for many masonry repairs. Make sure the one you choose matches the color of the material you're working on.

Before using any of these products, a few precautions are in order. First, ask the dealer if the product color will match concrete or mortar colors. Some of the products are white and make an unsightly patch. Next, try to line up enough crack repairs to use up all the patching in the tube or tubes you buy. The product is hard to store once it is opened. Finally, keep in mind that it's almost impossible to make a permanent repair in masonry because of the expansion and contraction factors we mentioned earlier. As seasons change, the cracks will open up again. Just think of an annual foray with caulk as routine maintenance.

49 Frost Line Requirements

A common question shared by many homeowners concerns the proper depth to dig post holes and foundations for outdoor projects. The most frequent response is to dig the hole down to the *frost line*, the depth to which the soil freezes in your locale. (The reason for the advice to dig to the frost line is that frozen ground heaves or expands, and will raise any structure whose base is not below the depth where the ground freezes.) Generally speaking, this advice is good, but one problem with it is that the frost line varies geographically. In my own Minnesota, for example, the frost line is 48 inches deep, whereas in the far West or deep South, there is no frost line because these areas have no prolonged freezing weather. To find the right depth for holes or foundation trenches in your area, call your local building department or inspector.

Keeping regional differences in mind, here are a few general guidelines: Most free-standing structures with wooden floors should have posts or foundations that extend to the frost line. A gazebo, for example, should have footings at the frost line, so the frost will not heave it unevenly and leave the building out of plumb. The posts that rest on the footings and that support the gazebo can extend down to the frost line, with concrete or tamped gravel packed in the holes around the posts. Or you can form and pour concrete piers that reach to the frost line, and set the posts or joists atop the concrete piers—above the surface of the ground—anchored there by metal concrete-to-wood connectors.

A shed or garage that rests on a concrete slab floor, on the other hand, need not have frost footings below the frost line. The slab can be poured at grade, after the vegetation is removed and rock or gravel are spread to provide drainage under the slab. This type of construction is called a *floating slab*, and it is commonly used, even in Minnesota. The recommended procedure for floating concrete slabs is to dig a slight trench, perhaps 2 feet wide and 12 to 18 inches deep, so that the concrete pour is thicker at the perimeter of the slab. This will help prevent the slab from cracking on the edges where the weight of the framed building will rest.

If a deck is attached to the side of the house on a ledger board, the outboard posts—those that hold up the far end of the deck—need not necessarily be dug to frost depth. The house side of the deck will not heave or raise in any event, because it is attached to the house itself.

However, if the deck edge is more than 3 feet above ground level, you should sink the posts deeper to resist the increased wind load.

Note that metal connectors can be used to anchor wood to concrete piers for most structures. If the post holes you require are for fence posts, you should never use metal connectors above the ground. Rather, the fence posts should be set into the ground to anchor the fence against high-wind pressures from the sides. The rule for fence posts is to set the post in the ground to a depth equal to one-third of the post height aboveground. For example, a fence that will be 6 feet tall should have 2 feet of post in the ground. Keep in mind that the new fast-set, no-mix concrete products are excellent for anchoring fence posts.

Remember to check with your local building department and any contractors you may know to determine the common building practices in your area. And when in doubt, realize that it's always better to go too deep than too shallow.

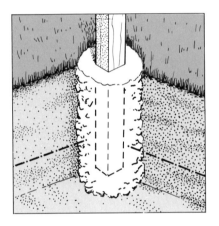

The frost line (dotted line) is the depth that freezing temperatures will reach in any area. Footings should be below the frost line.

50 Patching Blacktop

Blacktop (asphalt) driveways require more maintenance than concrete ones because the asphalt tends to lose oils from exposure to the direct sunlight, causing it to dry out and crack. As tiny cracks develop and fill with fall rains, the water freezes and expands in the cracks, breaking up the blacktop. Depending on the climate where you live, blacktop may need patching and sealing on an annual basis.

Not so many years ago, there were no patch products available for do-it-yourselfers. The homeowner could visit the asphalt plant and carry home hot asphalt in galvanized garbage cans to do one's own patching, or one could hire pros to do it. Now, *cold patch* products for large areas are widely available, as well as crack patching compounds and sealers in 5-gallon pails.

The first step in blacktop repair is to clean the surface with a driveway cleaner. This will remove any dirt and oil from the surface. Let the slab dry, then patch any cracks using the caulk tube patchers. A good tip to remember is that you can save on patching expenses if you partially fill deep cracks with sand before applying the patcher.

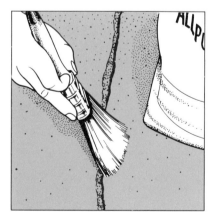

To fill cracks in asphalt, first remove any debris, then partially fill with fine sand to reduce the amount of patching needed.

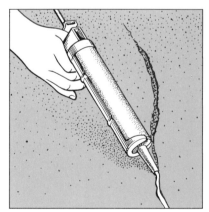

Load the patching compound into a caulk gun, then fill the crack. Use a putty knife, dipped in solvent, to smooth the patch.

Even though cold patching products are called *cold*, in contrast to the hot asphalt mix the pros use, it's a good idea to let all asphalt repair products stand in the sun for several hours, so they will thin out and become easier to spread and smooth on the driveway.

When all cracks and holes have been filled, use a squeegee and broom to spread the sealer. Spread the sealer at the recommended rate of coverage. Heavy-duty sealers are available at higher cost, but in harsh northern climates this heavier product doesn't seem to reduce the number of coats or the amount of maintenance needed.

51 Renewing a Deck Surface

Every deck surface takes a beating because it catches the full brunt of both blistering sunlight and rain or snow. Inspect your deck each spring because regular maintenance will help it survive longer and look better.

The first step is to check between deck boards for leaves, twigs, and other debris that might hold moisture. The deck must drain quickly after a rain. Standing water or constant wetting will destroy any wood species.

Next, go over the deck with a hammer and a nailset, driving in any nails that may have popped above the surface. This step will keep your deck strong and smooth. (Popped nails become loose, rust, then fail.) If necessary, renail any loose areas with galvanized or aluminum nails to avoid future rust.

If the deck boards are split or splintered, sand them smooth or replace them. Then apply a coat of your favorite deck finish. If you're undecided about what to use, look for a stain and sealer product that will wear well, has ultraviolet blockers to block out the sun's rays, contains a mildewcide, and is warranted to last two years or more between coats.

Use a paint roller with a long-nap fleece cover that will reach into all the cracks and crannies for full coverage. A helpful aid to save your back is to buy an extension handle for the roller, so you can place the roller pan on the deck and work while standing.

One hard-to-reach area is the drain spaces between deck boards. Buy a couple of disposable sponge brushes for staining the edges in the cracks between the boards. The sponges can reach down into the cracks to ensure full stain protection of the wood.

When refinishing a deck, apply the new coating to the wide areas with a roller. But use a small sponge brush to cover the edges.

52 Painting Wrought Iron

Wrought-iron railings and trim can add a design plus to any house. But they can be time-consuming to paint because the intricate shapes and patterns make preparation and coating difficult. One way to make the preparation easier is to use a rotary wire brush chucked into an electric drill. This can clean rust and dirt from wrought iron much quicker than a handheld wire brush.

And, when it's time to paint, try a variety of flexible painting tools, including the rollers that are specially designed to clamp over ironwork and roll both sides at the same time. While these hand tools do have their advantages, probably the best job is achieved using aerosol paint.

The flat-black finish that is representative of true wrought iron is available in aerosol cans. And, the spray can be readily directed for full coverage of intricate shapes. Before using it, however, you should apply masking tape and paper to any surrounding surfaces. And only spray paint on calm days to avoid windblown paint damage.

To prepare wrought iron for painting, brush off any rust or flaking paint. Then wipe the surface with mineral spirits.

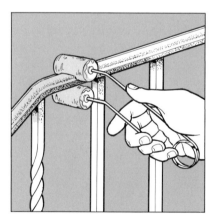

Use a special roller, like the one shown, or an aerosol spray can to paint the ironwork. A flat-black finish is the traditional look.

53 Cleaning Retaining Walls

To clean any exterior wood, apply deck cleaner and let it soak until the surface is sudsy. Then thoroughly rinse it and let dry.

Once the surface is dry, apply wood sealer using a roller or spray gun. Reseal whenever water drops stop forming on the surface.

New products abound for cleaning wood decks. But keep in mind that these cleaners will also work to clean other wood structures, such as fences and timber retaining walls. Check the label of the cleaner before you buy it. Some of these cleaners are so versatile they can even be used to clean your fiberglass boat or to remove oxidized paint from aluminum siding and other surfaces.

To use these cleaners, first mix with water according to the label directions. Most cleaners are concentrated and can be mixed 1 gallon of cleaner to 4 or more gallons of clean water. Be sure to wear rubber gloves and eye protection when mixing or applying any chemicals.

Use a garden hose or a pressure washer to wet down the wood, then apply the wood cleaner using a stiff scrub brush. Make sure that you brush the entire surface with the cleaning solution. Then let the cleaner set for a few minutes, and rescrub any stubborn areas if necessary. When the cleaner is working, a foam will appear on the wood.

When the cleaner has lifted the dirt, flush the wall with water. Then let the timber wall dry, and check to be sure you have removed all grime and any mildew. If necessary, repeat the cleaning, and when the timbers are dry, apply a wood sealer.

Some sealers are the consistency of water and can be sprayed on using a garden sprayer. Others require a roller with a long nap. Be sure you cover all the rough wood surface and apply enough sealer to soak thoroughly into the wood. To maintain the wall in the future, periodically rinse it with clean water. When water appears to soak into the wood and no longer forms beads on the wall surface, it's time to clean again and apply a fresh coat of sealer.

54 Chalked Paint

A common homeowner query is: What kind of paint should I use over chalked paint? Most often the advice is to use oil paint on a chalked surface, but the answer should be: Don't paint over chalked paint—clean it. In the past, chalking was very difficult to remove from house siding or trim, but many of the new deck-cleaning products will remove it.

To clean your siding, first wash off any visible dirt or grime, and then mix up some cleaner. Be sure to wear long pants, a long-sleeved shirt, eye protection, and rubber gloves when working with this or any harmful chemicals. Keep in mind that the deck cleaner is concentrated, so you should mix it according to label directions, usually about 4 or 5 parts water to 1 part cleaner. You may have to use a scrub brush to remove the chalked paint, and a pressure washer is great for power-flushing the surface after you've loosened the chalked particles.

If the chalked paint is still a problem, you can stabilize it using a product called Emulsa-Bond made by the Flood Company (P.O. Box 399, Hudson, Ohio 44236). This product was designed to act as a binder to lock down the fine chalked particles. Once you've coated the chalked surface with Emulsa-Bond—according to the manufacturer's directions—you can topcoat it with any latex or oil product you want.

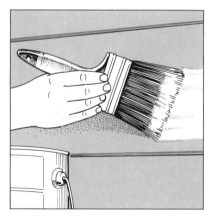

To stabilize chalked paint, first wash the surface with deck cleaner, then apply a primer, and follow with latex or oil paint.

Remember, the advice to use only oil or alkyd paints on chalked surfaces ignores the advances in paint technology. Modern acrylic latex products work very well on chalked surfaces and will hold up well. Two excellent examples are Benjamin Moore's Exterior Latex and Olympic's Overcoat paint, both of which are usually available at your local paint dealers.

55 Keeping It Clean

In these days of increased concern over environmental pollution from chemicals, the power washer has become an even more welcome tool for home maintenance. There are few dirty surfaces that will not come clean if subjected to a water stream of 800 pounds or more of pressure. These tools are common rental items, often by the half day, and a half day may be adequate for doing all your exterior spring cleaning.

If the surface to be cleaned is very dirty, or covered with mildew, you can first soak it with a spray of diluted chlorine bleach. Mix the bleach 50/50 with clean water, then apply the bleach with the washer unit or a pump-type garden sprayer. If the surface isn't all that dirty, you may need only to apply a fine mist to presoak and loosen the dirt. Let the water or bleach-and-water solution set on the surface for a while, until it loosens the grime. Then, turn the sprayer unit up to full pressure, and blast away dirt and mildew. It is best to pressure wash on a hot day because the surface will dry quickly and permit you to inspect it to make sure it's clean. If not, keep washing. Use the washer on house siding, eaves, soffits, porch ceilings, driveways, sidewalks, retaining walls, and decks.

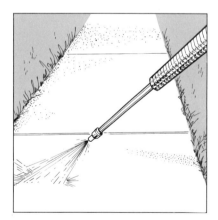

For stubborn stains on driveways, garage floors, and sidewalks, presoak the surface with driveway cleaner, then pressure wash.

Instead of a costly and time-consuming painting job, sometimes all your house needs is a thorough cleaning with a power washer.

56 Combating Carpenter Ants

Anyone who thinks pressure-treated lumber will resist attack from insects like carpenter ants never met the ants that inhabit our retaining wall. These ants grew fat and happy from feeding on the ground-side timbers. Each season they deposited finely chewed sawdust along the joints in our retaining wall. No amount of ant poison would deter them. We even suspected that several pesticides acted like ant vitamins instead—so large and vigorous did the ants become.

In desperation, we sprayed some Ortho Hornet & Wasp spray between the timbers of the retaining wall. The immediate result was no more ants. They completely abandoned our wall.

Carpenter ants attack any wood structure, including retaining walls. As soon as you see them, spray the area with pesticide.

Once all the ants have died, immediately sprinkle diazinon around the perimeter of the wall. This will help stop reinfestation.

57 Cleaning Siding

Aluminum siding carries the happy guarantee that it won't need painting. This is true, up to a point, because factory-applied aluminum finishes do last a long while, up to 20 years in many cases. Of course, no finish lasts indefinitely. Air pollution and acid rain increasingly are causing premature paint failure. A common sight is siding with a finish that has oxidized, leaving the paint film intact but dull.

To clean oxidized paint from metal siding, use one of the products made to clean outdoor decks. Check the product label to see if it's recommended for cleaning prefinished metal siding. If so, just mix the concentrated cleaner with water, at the ratio recommended on the label, and prewet the siding with a spray nozzle or pressure sprayer. Then use an automotive-type sponge to apply the cleaner and to rinse away dirt or oxidized paint. It's best to use two pails and two sponges for this chore: one pail filled with cleaner, the other pail filled with clean water. It's easier to wash away the fine paint particles while the siding is still wet. The more water pressure you can use, the better.

58 Repairing Concrete Steps

The corners on concrete steps tend to get cracked and damaged over the winter. This was once a tough repair, but today's concrete bonding products help make the job easier and increase the odds of a long-lasting patch.

First, using a steel-wire brush, remove the loose concrete particles, working down to a firm surface. Next, apply a latex bonding liquid to the repair area (some concrete patch products contain this adhesive). In a cardboard mixing pail, available at your paint store, mix the concrete patch material. Use a paint scraper or trowel to apply the patch. Build up the patch until it's shaped roughly like the corner.

After the first application of concrete patch, place the wood form on the corner as shown, holding it in place with duct tape. Coat the inside of the form with oil to keep it from sticking to the concrete. Fill the form with concrete patch until you've built up a smooth, even corner.

While the concrete is still wet but firm, smooth the repair with a wet paintbrush. This also helps fill small voids in the concrete. Set up a ladder or other barrier to keep people off the step until the patch is dry and hard, usually overnight.

Clean away debris on damaged concrete with a wire brush. Concrete patch will bond poorly unless corner is prepared.

Use a paintbrush to apply concrete bonding adhesive to the damaged area. A synthetic bristle brush works best here.

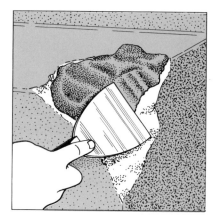

Mix concrete patch in a disposable paint bucket, using a paint stirring stick. Apply patch with a flat knife.

Tape form around the corner. Pack remaining patch into the form and leave the form in place until patch is dry.

Remove form and smooth over patch with a wet paintbrush. Avoid patch until it is fully hardened in a few days.

59 Stucco Renewal

In warmer areas of the United States where temperatures never drop below freezing, masonry paints are sometimes used to renew stucco that has grown dingy with time. But in northern states, moisture migration through walls that have no vapor barriers will often cause widespread paint failures, such as peeling and mildew. Stucco is in fact a masonry finish; thus, any finish coat applied over it should be a nonsealing masonry product.

If you have stucco that is aged, first try power-washing it. Grime and mildew that can collect on the stucco make it look dull and dirty. Washing will often bring back the new stucco look. Use a garden sprayer or a power washer to apply a masonry cleaning product to the stucco. First, wash with clear water to wet the stucco and begin soaking dirt loose. Then apply a cleaner. You can use a 50/50 mix of water and ordinary chlorine bleach, or ask your hardware store to recommend a cleaner for masonry. Be sure to rinse the entire surface thoroughly with clean water.

The first choice for renewing stucco should be a cement-base stucco coating. These are available in dry form and must be mixed with water. Most manufacturers offer several color choices. Thoro, for example, offers a color chart of 10 stucco colors. Mix the stucco according to direc-

For small repairs, first clean the surface, then mix the stucco according to the label directions. Apply it with a sponge or a roller.

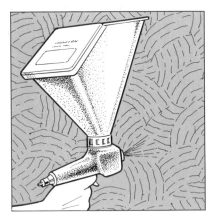

For larger stucco repairs, you can rent a hopper-type spray gun. These tools have different orifices for a variety of masonry finishes.

tions on the bag, and apply over the old stucco using a rental hopper-type sprayer or a sponge, brush, or roller.

If you choose to use paint on stucco, tell your paint dealer of your intentions, and ask for advice on which paint product is best and for proper application techniques. Also, ask for the address of any houses that have been painted with the product, and visit them, if possible, to see how the product has performed.

CHAPTER SIX

101

LAWN
AND
GARDEN

TIPS

60 Reviving Damaged Lawns

It's not unusual to find areas of dead grass on your lawn in the springtime. These dead spots may be the result of snow being shoveled or plowed in deep piles along the driveway or street. Heavy, compacted snow, and salt and other chemicals used to melt ice or snow kill small areas of grass. Fortunately, if these areas are attended to early in the growing season, they should be strong enough to withstand the withering weeks of late July and August.

To repair these damaged areas, wait until the ground is soft after a rain or watering, then scrape away the dead grass with a garden fork. Next, prepare the spot by loosening up the top layer of soil. Rake the soil smooth. Ask your lawn and garden dealer to recommend a gypsum soil conditioner, and apply it to the areas according to the product's label directions.

Next, reseed and fertilize the area, or cover it with sod. Sod is good to use on slopes, where seeds are liable to be washed away. Avoid walking on the grass and cutting it until you are sure it has firmly taken hold. Whether you sod or seed the area, water the patched area well daily to get the grass off to a good start.

Water the damaged turf, or wait until after a rain when ground is soft, to remove old grass from damaged spot.

Remove enough dead grass and soil so sod can be fitted into patch. Cut the sod to fit using an old kitchen knife.

Spread potting soil around patch to fill gaps and level the joint between old and new grass. Keep the sod watered.

61 Winter Plant Storage

Many people have several hundred dollars worth of yard and deck plants. Not only are these plants expensive, but they require several seasons to reach good size and full growth. If you live in the North, you cannot leave such plants outside in the winter. But you can store them in your basement under fluorescent lights from mid-October to the end of April.

Many plants will sit on makeshift shelves constructed from scrap lumber and concrete blocks. Hanging plants can be hooked over nails driven in the floor joists above.

Shop lights are often on sale for $10 each or less, and the fluorescent bulbs cost about $1 each. Even the cost for electricity to operate them is only pennies per month. But, the rewards of saving the plants are many, including having a crop of healthy, bushy plants that flowers on your deck each spring.

To save deck and yard plants from year to year, store them in the basement during the winter with shop lights turned on overhead.

62 Painting Chain-Link Fences

Chain-link fencing has a durable galvanized coating that keeps it trouble-free for years. Eventually, even this galvanizing will fail, and the fence will require painting.

Wire fencing can be difficult to paint. Brushing on paint is usually slow and tedious, while spraying the open fencing permits too much wasted paint from overspray. The best solution is to use a long-nap paint roller. The long nap reaches into the weave of the wire and covers hard-to-reach corners. And, it's a good idea to enlist your neighbor to paint his side of the fence while you paint yours. This way, you will see each others' misses and can touch up the paint as you go.

Before starting, use a rotary wire brush, chucked into a drill, to clean away loose rust or dirt. You can also use an ordinary wire brush to clean the surface. When everything is properly prepared, wipe down the fence with a sponge that's been soaked in mineral spirits. When the fence is dry, apply the paint. Aluminum paint is a common choice for restoring chain link, or you can use any color paint. Just be sure to use paint designed for covering metal, not woods.

To paint the wire panels on a typical chain-link fence, use a long-nap paint roller. The long nap reaches into the tight bends.

63 Painting a Wood Fence

Wood fences—such as the privacy fence shown here—often have offset boards that defy ordinary painting methods. If the board fence is also made of rough-sawn lumber, such as cedar or pine, the paint tool of choice should be a sprayer.

The hand-held cup sprayer shown is a reasonable tool if the fence is not too large. But a gun cup system can be a nuisance if you have a lot of fence to cover and gallons of paint or stain to apply. Refilling its quart-sized reservoir gets tiring very fast. Instead, consider renting an airless sprayer with a suction tube that can be used with any size container.

Keep in mind that airborne paint particles can become windblown and cause spatter problems for your neighbors. The repercussions can be legally and financially depressing. To control paint overspray, heed the following list of tips:

- Do not spray paint on windy days. Wind can carry paint droplets far from the work area. Wait for calm weather to paint.

- Check the opposite side of the fence and be sure that there is no car, lawn equipment, or other object near the fence. Ask your neighbor to move everything of value from the area.

The easiest way to paint a fence is with a spray painter. To control overspray, drape a plastic sheet over opposite side of fence.

- Buy plastic sheeting and staple it so it drapes over the opposite side of the fence. When you paint the backside of the fence, remove the sheeting and cover your own side of the fence so that airborne paint is stopped before it can travel or become windblown.

- Finally, don't overthin your paint or stain.

64 Trash Bag Composting

Composting grass clippings need not be a smelly business, nor take months to complete. If you have small amounts of grass, just place them in plastic lawn bags. Add 1 cup of high-nitrogen fertilizer to each bag, sprinkle water on top, and seal it with a twist-tie. Roll the bag over to mix the water fertilizer, and grass clippings. Then place the bag or bags in a storage shed or garage. Try to roll them over once or more frequently if you like. Within a couple of months, you will have rich compost that you can spread on your garden, use to nourish new trees, or mix with perlite to make potting soil.

For quick composting of your grass clippings, place clippings in trash bag, add fertilizer and water, then seal and turn frequently.

65 Removing Troublesome Ivy

In Grandpa's day, sentimentalists wrote songs about the joys of living in a vine-covered cottage. Anyone who ever had to paint one of those cottages knows that ivy is something less than a real joy: You can't paint around it, and it's *very* difficult to remove. Ivy is held in place by tiny-but-tough hairlike tendrils. These tendrils invade every available crack and cranny, where they are almost impossible to pry out, especially on masonry walls. In addition, water can penetrate into the tiny cracks that have been formed by these tendrils causing damage during each freeze-and-thaw cycle.

To remove the ivy from masonry surfaces, start by cutting apart the vines and pulling them from the wall. Be sure to wear gloves to keep from injuring your hands. (You can use a scraper to remove the tendrils that cling to smooth siding.) Then use a propane torch to burn off the tips of the tendrils and get rid of all vegetation. Remember to keep a hose and spray nozzle handy, and spray down any surface that was hit with the flame. Take special care if you decide to burn off the tendrils from wood siding. Spray the siding as soon as the ivy is removed, and then keep watch for several hours to be sure there is no possibility of starting a house fire.

Use pruning shears to cut the bulk of the ivy from the wall. Then follow up with a simple paint scraper or stiff wire brush.

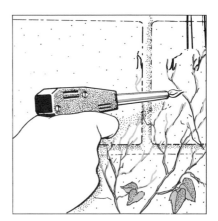

Burn off stubborn tendrils with a propane torch and brush away any residue. Keep a hose handy when working with the flame.

66 Drought-Free Lawn

To check how much water your lawn is getting from your sprinkler, place a couple of open pails around the yard to act as gauges.

Perhaps you live in an area where watering the lawn is often prohibited, or rising water bills make you think twice about the expense of watering. Here are some steps you can take that will help you keep the lawn green and healthy, but let you use less water.

The first step for conserving water is to mulch everything. Buy or rent a shredder to turn lawn waste into mulch. Spread a layer at least 4 to 6 inches thick around trees, shrubs, and in flower or vegetable gardens. Mulch helps hold moisture, reduces moisture loss from evaporation in hot weather, and discourages weed growth. Making and using mulch can also reduce the amount of lawn waste you generate, important in these days of overloaded landfills.

The average lawn needs about 1 inch of water per week to keep grass green and healthy. This includes whatever rainfall you've had during the period. Keep track of the rainfall in your area for two weeks, then water your lawn enough to bring the total up to 2 inches. If you have an underground sprinkler system, of course, it will have a meter that will let you gauge exactly how much water you want to apply to your lawn. If you use a hose and sprinklers, you can paint marks inside plastic pails or coffee cans at 1- and 2-inch levels. Set these around the lawn and check when you have the right water depth in the containers. Then shut off the hose to avoid wasting water.

Another thing you can do to reduce lawn water usage in hot weather is to set your mower blade height at 2 inches. Taller grass will reduce evaporation from the soil by shading it more. On very hot days, sprinkle the lawn lightly at sundown. This practice, called *syringing*, cools the lawn and helps the grass survive on less water.

67 Fixing Lawn Furniture

Last year's wooden garden furniture may have looked pretty good when you picked it out in the store. Now that it's been through a season, you may have found that poor construction, or simple heavy-duty relaxing, has taken its toll. What once seemed like a sturdy piece of outdoor equipment now greets you with a wobble and a groan. Upon close inspection, you may find that the wooden joints are simply held together with staples or small nails. However, you can make your wooden furniture last for several more seasons with this tip.

Stop by the hardware store and check out the wide assortment of steel reinforcing brackets. These come in T and L shapes and are secured with flathead wood screws. Pick out the brackets that are suitable for reinforcing the joints on your wooden lawn furniture.

Install the metal brackets at all key stress points. Use them to strengthen crossbraces, where the arms meet the back and on parts that are suspended by chains or ropes. Be sure to use galvanized screws that are sized for the stock you're fastening and that have heads that fit neatly in the metal reinforcing brackets. If you're beefing up a new piece of unfinished wooden lawn furniture, install the brackets before you apply the finish.

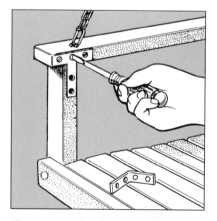

If your wooden lawn furniture isn't sturdily built, reinforce the joints at all key stress points with metal brackets.

68 Sharpening Garden Tools

Farmers know about the value of sharp tools for the garden, but many city folks will bring a garden hoe or shovel home and go right to work with them, never thinking to sharpen them first. The work goes much easier with sharp tools, especially when summer sun makes soil dry and hard. Keep a file or grinder handy in your toolshed, and sharpen your tools frequently. Hand shears, garden hoes, shovels, spades, and mower blades are just a few of the tools that need to be sharpened before they're put into service, and then kept sharp as you use them.

Another trick farmers know is to fill a 5-gallon pail with fine sand, then pour a quart or two of waste oil from the lawn mower into the sand. When you finish using the tool, work the tool blade up and down in the oil-soaked sand. This will remove dirt from the blade and leave an oil coating that will prevent rust on tool blades. Finally, sand the wood handles lightly to smooth raised grain, to make the handle blister-free and to extend its life.

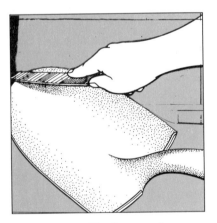

Garden tools, like hoes and shovels, work much better when they're sharp. To sharpen them, use a hand-held file or grinding stone.

69 Lawn Mower Tuneup

You don't have to be a professional mechanic to give your lawn mower a preseason tuneup. If your mower won't start, it's usually one of three things: the spark plug is fouled, the air filter is clogged, or the carburetor is dirty.

Unlike your car, which has multiple spark plugs, your lawn mower has only one. Because small-engine spark plugs work so hard, they frequently become fouled. Buy several spark plugs at once. Clean or replace the plug at the first sign of poor starting.

First, remove the ignition wire from the plug, then use a socket wrench to remove the plug. Check the plug's electrode to be sure it is not burned or dirty. Clean the plug's electrode with fine sandpaper, or replace it. Leave the plug disconnected.

Unscrew the bolt that holds the air cleaner. Take the top off the cleaner, and remove the air filter element. Replace it or clean it in warm water and detergent, and squeeze it dry.

Next, spray a cleaner such as Gum-Out over the carburetor and its linkage. Lightly oil the control cables and linkage, and reinstall the air filter.

Next, remove the oil drain plug (near the shaft and mower blade) and change the oil. Drain the old oil into a pan and return it for recycling.

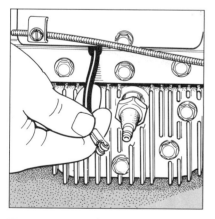

To prevent accidentally starting the mower, begin tuneup by removing the ignition wire from the spark plug.

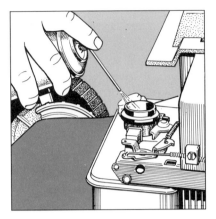

Use a screwdriver to loosen the slotted bolt that holds the air cleaner. Clean the filter element or replace it.

Spray aerosol cleaner such as Gum-Out into carburetor throat and on linkage. Lightly oil linkage after cleaning it.

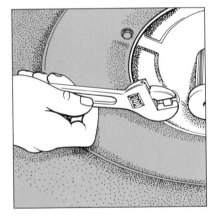

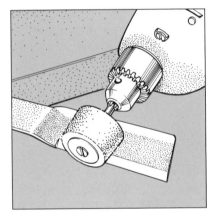

To drain oil from mower, remove the drain plug on the underside of the mower deck. Refill crankcase with fresh oil.

Sharpen the mower blade with an abrasive drum chucked in an electric drill. If blade is badly nicked, replace it.

CHAPTER SEVEN

101 WALLS, CEILINGS, AND FLOORS TIPS

Patching Plaster

Most cracks in plaster are caused by movement in the building's structure. If you simply fill the cracks, it's likely that they'll open again within a short time. Also, the usual advice to undercut a crack so the patch will hold better is unwise. The patch may not fall out, but there's nothing to keep the crack from reappearing. To do the job right, reinforce the patch with paper drywall tape. First, scrape away any loose plaster from the area. Then cover the crack with drywall compound, embed the tape, and wipe away the excess compound with a taping knife. When the compound is dry, apply a thin cover coat of compound. After this coat is dry, add a second, very thin coat and, when dry, smooth by wet sanding.

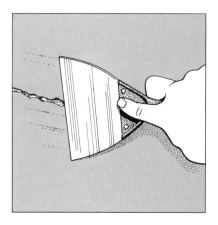

Use a taping knife to clean away loose particles or projecting plaster chips from the crack and the surrounding area.

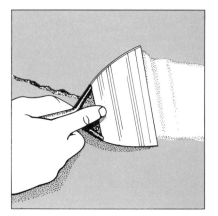

Next, apply a coat of premixed drywall taping compound over the repair area. Use a 4- or 6-inch-wide taping knife.

Embed paper drywall tape into the compound, centering the tape over the crack. Wipe away excess and let dry.

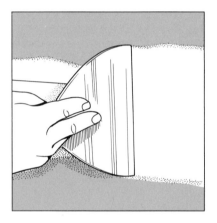

Apply a very thin coat of compound to cover the tape. After it's dry, apply a second thin coat and sand smooth.

71 Drying a Patch

When decorating, waiting for plaster drywall or patching compound to dry can be a frustration. Here are a few tips for speeding up the process.

First, choose your patching materials wisely. Compounds with a latex base will usually dry within a few hours at most. Patch plaster sets quickly, but takes longer to dry. If you use patch plaster to fill deep holes, you can use drywall compound for a smooth topcoat. Very small holes filled with spackle will be dry enough for priming the same day.

For extensive repairs, use a quick-set drywall compound such as Sta-Smooth or Durabond. These will set in as little as 45 minutes. Fast-setting compounds are harder to work with, however. Mix only small amounts at a time, and use a plastic pail for mixing. When the job is done, allow the waste to harden in the pail, and then flex the sides to break it loose. Keep your tools clean, and do not pour compound or wash water down your drains where it can set and harden in the pipes.

Finally, use warm water to hasten drying, or force-dry the patch with a hair dryer or electric heat gun. With latex paint, you needn't wait until the patch is completely dry.

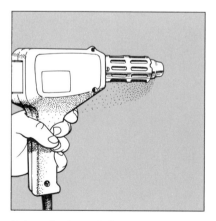

Using the hot air from an electric heat gun or hair dryer is one way to speed up drying time of wall-patching compounds.

72 Cutting Patches

If you've ever had to cut multiples of the same shape from cloth or paper, you know that the easy way to do the job is to double up the material and cut two or more pieces simultaneously. Called double cutting, this method can also be used to cut repair patches for wallcoverings or vinyl floors, so they fit precisely and the patterns are exactly aligned.

To repair a small damaged section, first position a scrap piece of matching material over the affected area. Align the patch material so its pattern lines up perfectly with that on the original material. Then tape the repair piece in place with masking tape so it won't shift while it's being cut.

Next, use a razor knife to cut a shape through both the patch and the original material. Always use a sharp, new blade so you can cut through both layers without forcing the tool or slipping. Keep the blade held at right angles to the surface so the patch and repair cutout will be exactly the same size. If there are lines in the pattern, make your cuts on these lines to better conceal the patch. If there are no pattern lines, make an irregular cutout with wavy lines so the cutline will be less visible.

Remove the patch and use water, solvent, or heat—depending on the adhesive used—to soften the glue under the damaged section, and then

Damage to most any material that can be cut with a razor knife, such as torn wallpaper, can be repaired by double cutting.

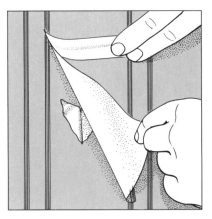

Cut a patch from scrap material so it's slightly larger than the damaged area. Tape it in place so its pattern is aligned.

remove it. If you're working with thick material, pry up the section slowly and check that you've cut all the way through. If necessary, carefully deepen the cut. Apply adhesive to the back of the patch, insert it into the hole, and carefully adjust its position so it fits exactly. Press the patch firmly in place, and use a sponge dampened with the appropriate solvent to wipe away excess adhesive from the patch and surrounding area.

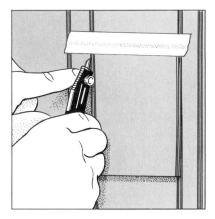

Use a sharp razor knife to cut both layers at once. Align cut with pattern lines, or use a wavy cutline if there's no pattern.

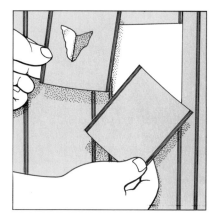

Use water to loosen glue under wallpaper. Carefully remove damaged section and check that your patch fits.

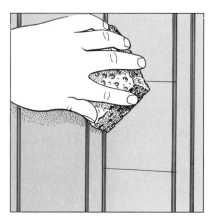

Apply glue to patch back and carefully locate in hole. Use a sponge to smooth patch and remove any excess adhesive.

73 Painting Paneling

To paint paneling, first sand the entire surface using 120-grit paper. An orbital finishing sander will make the job go much faster.

With sanding done and dust removed, apply an alkyd primer with a low-nap roller. Oil base or latex paint can be used for top coat.

If you've inherited a roomful of dark wood paneling, or have simply grown tired of the finish, you can paint over it to lighten the room or change the color. As with most materials, paint success depends primarily on proper preparation.

The first step is to scuff-sand the gloss finish to give the paint a better surface to grab. Use a power sander or sanding block and 120-grit sandpaper. Then fill any nail holes or other blemishes with a high-quality wood filler. Once the filler is dry, sand the patches smooth.

When you are done sanding, remove the dust and then apply an alkyd primer to the surface and let it dry. You can finish coat with the paint of your choice, either latex or alkyd. But for the best results, use a low-nap paint roller to apply the paint to the paneling.

74 Wallcovering Tips

Most of the wallcovering installed today is not *paper*, it's vinyl. And most of the wallcovering is now prepasted, not plain, to save the homeowner the task of mixing and applying adhesive. In early days, there were some failures with the prepasted coverings, and, although manufacturers have made great strides in adhesive technology, you can still hear complaints about coverings that didn't stay put.

There are several ways to ensure that prepasted wallcoverings do stay put, have closed seams, and do not blister or loosen from the wall. The first step is to prime the wall with an alkyd primer, which seals the wall so moisture cannot soak from the adhesive into the drywall or plaster.

Another tip is to control the temperature and the humidity in the space where you will be working. Close the windows, shut the doors, and turn off the thermostats on heating equipment to keep the room cool and draft-free. If the day is very hot and dry, place throw rugs under the cracks at the bottom of the doors and run a humidifier in the room to raise the humidity and to slow the drying time. This will prevent premature drying of the adhesive and will increase your *open time*—the time you have to fit and smooth the wallcovering before the adhesive sets.

If you're worried about prepasted wallpaper sticking to the wall, coat its backside with a water and paste solution before hanging.

If you still mistrust the prepasted coverings, buy an adhesive intended for use with vinyl coverings. Add 1 quart of vinyl adhesive to 1 gallon of warm water. Lay the wallcovering strips on a table and, instead of dipping the strips in a water tray, use a paint roller with a medium nap to apply the mix to the covering. The water will activate the glue on the back of the covering, and adding the quart of adhesive to the solution will provide added assurance that the coverings will stay put. Don't neglect, however, to inspect the seams after the covering has hung awhile. Any shrinkage can be adjusted if you do it while the piece is still wet.

75 Painting Over Wall Stains

If your budding artist has used your wall for a canvas, your first impulse may be to try to paint over the stain. But many stains cannot be covered with paint alone: Rust, grease or oil, crayon wax, and magic-marker ink may be activated by the solvent (water or oil) in the paint, and bleed back through the new paint. This is true regardless of how many coats of paint you apply. You must either seal over the stain or remove it from the wall before painting.

Many decorating texts will advise you to just seal the stain in. The problem with this approach is that if you apply a good sealer—such as shellac—over the stain, the new paint will be shinier over the patch than it is over the rest of the wall. Depending on where they're located, these shiny patches can be unsightly.

The best approach is to try to remove the stain. Check with your local paint dealer for products with trade names such as *Lift Off*. These cleaners contain solvents that will remove spattered latex paints, grease, crayons, or other stains. To use them, pour some cleaner on a clean cloth, wet the stain, and let the cleaner work for a couple of minutes. If you just try to scrub the stain away, you may remove the wall paint with the stain. Wiping gently will minimize damage to the finish.

If the stain comes off, then just prime and paint normally. But if the stain remains, coat it with shellac first, then paint over it.

Before painting over stains, make every effort to remove them. Try different removers until you find one that works on your stain.

If the stain comes off the paint, spot-prime the stain area and then repaint the wall. If it proves difficult to remove, you can seal in almost any stain with a shellac sealer. Shellac is fast-drying so it does not activate the stain material, and is especially effective over rust and grease. It is also useful for sealing over smoke and oil stains, which are common after a house fire.

To avoid the shiny spots due to higher sheen over the shellac sealer, seal the entire wall with shellac, not just the stain.

76 Finding Studs

To hang heavy objects on the wall, you must locate the wall studs. Draperies, large pictures, and mirrors must be hung on anchors fastened to the wood framing, not simply driven into wallboard or plaster. With a little detective work, you can easily locate wall studs or other framing members.

If you have wallboard on your walls, finding the studs is easy. Turn off all lights in the room and remove the shade from a lamp, or use a bare bulb in a trouble light. Hold the bare bulb close to the wall, just far enough away so the heat from the bulb will not scorch the wall. With this strong sidelight, you should be able to see the slight indentations over the nail- or screwheads. Each row of these fasteners marks a stud location.

Another way to locate the studs is to check the baseboard along the bottom of the wall. The nails used to attach baseboards are usually driven into the wall studs. Once you locate these nails, measure the distance from them to the nearest wall. Then measure the same distance near the top of the wall. A straight line between the two will represent the length of the hidden stud.

Also, stud locaters—which are available in two basic types—work well. One has a magnetized arrow inside a clear window in the locater.

Electronic stud finders are a great way to locate framing members hidden in a wall or ceiling. They measure density differences.

To use it, just move the tool laterally across the wall. The magnetic arrow will move when the locater goes over a nail in the wall. The nail, of course, indicates the location of a wood stud.

Electronic stud locaters work best. To use them, all you have to do is move the tool over a known stud location and note how it reads. The locater reveals the difference in density between the plaster or wallboard and the wood stud.

77 Run-Free Masking Tape

Have you ever masked an area such as wood trim only to find, upon removing the masking tape, that paint had seeped under the edge of the tape and onto the trim you were trying to protect? Here are a couple of tips to prevent loose edges on masking tape and ensure clean paint lines:

- When masking wood trim, wipe over the surface where you'll apply the tape with fine 0000 steel wool. This will remove any bumps caused by lint or dust that got stuck in the fresh paint on the last coat. Then run your hand over the area to be masked to be sure it's smooth, and wipe the trim with a clean cloth or tack rag to remove any dust that was caused by the steel wool.

- When the trim is clean and smooth, position the masking tape and press it in place. Now use the tip of a putty knife to run along the edge of the tape, to ensure a complete seal.

- Finally, be sure to remove the masking tape as soon as the paint is dry enough so it won't run (usually within 1 hour). This way, you can inspect your job for any runs and deal with them while they're still easy to clean. Just wrap a clean rag around the tip of the putty knife, dip the tip into water or another appropriate solvent, and wipe away the paint runs.

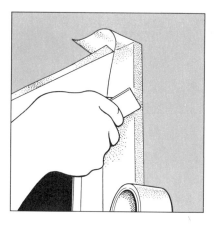

To keep paint from running under masking tape, rub the surface with steel wool, then press the tape in place with a putty knife.

78 Painting Cleanup

Try as you may, paintbrushes or rollers often don't come clean with washing, and the result is stiff brush bristles or a roller that's rock hard. It's difficult to get paint tools completely clean with soap and water alone, even though latex paint is a water-based product.

To thoroughly clean brushes and rollers, buy a cleaning tool that has teeth on one side and a curved edge on the other side. The curved side fits around a paint roller and helps force the paint from the nap. The toothed edge is used to comb the brush bristles after cleaning to keep them straight.

As a general rule, you should remove as much paint as possible before you wash the brush or roller. Then flush the paint from the tool, applying a high volume of water. When the tool appears to be clean, squeeze it in your hand. If you still see paint residue oozing out, apply a solvent such as mineral spirits or brush cleaner to the brush or roller. Mineral spirits or brush cleaner will help bring out any paint residue, even latex.

Also, if you do any amount of painting yourself, invest in a spinner tool. The spinner has a spiral shaft like a child's top, and spins at high speed as you work the handle quickly up and down. The tool's round shaft can hold a roller, and a clamp device on the end can hold a brush

To clean a paintbrush, first soak it in solvent. Then hold it in the end clamp of a spinner tool and spin it until the solvent is gone.

The same tool works for rollers. Just soak the roller in solvent, then slide the roller onto the tool and spin it completely dry.

handle for cleaning. Slip the roller or brush onto the spinner, and position the end of the tool in a 5-gallon plastic paint pail. Spin the tool as rapidly as possible. The centrifugal action will force the water and/or solvent from the paintbrush bristles or the roller nap, and your painting tools will dry soft and be ready for the next project.

Buying Wallboard

Most consumers are aware that wallboard can be bought in almost any length—from 8 to 12 feet long. But you will also see wallboard for sale in several different thicknesses, with ⅜-inch-thick wallboard being the thinnest and cheapest. Before picking up your bargain, you should understand the advantages and limitations of each panel thickness.

Wallboard that is only ⅜-inch thick does not meet code requirements for use as a primary wall. It has little fire resistance, sound resistance, or impact strength. These thin panels cannot be used for ceilings because they are not thick enough to support the weight of ceiling insulation without sagging between the ceiling joists. Use ⅜-inch-thick wallboard as a new finish surface over deteriorated plaster, as a backer board underneath wood paneling, or in double thicknesses to match older, ¾-inch-thick plaster when you are remodeling.

The industry standard is ½-inch-thick wallboard. This can be used on walls or ceilings, with framing spaced up to 24 inches on center. Keep in mind, however, that thicker and heavier insulation blankets in the attic can place extra weight on ceilings. Therefore, ⅝-inch-thick panels are preferred on ceilings, especially where trusses are spaced 24 inches on center.

Special applications also require ⅝-inch-thick wallboard. The thicker wall panels have better soundproofing qualities because they have extra mass and weight. These thicker panels also have extra fireproofing qualities. They have a fire rating of 60 minutes, compared to a 45-minute fire rating for ½-inch-thick wallboard.

80 Avoiding Nail Pops

Nail pops can occur any time that wood is nailed (or screwed) to wood or any other material. They are most common, and perhaps most objectionable, when they occur on interior wallboard, especially on ceilings that have bright light fixtures. But nail pops are also a visible nuisance on exterior siding. And, when they occur on decks, they are not only unattractive, they also present a hazard to bare skin.

What causes nail pops? It was once thought that nails simply become loose and move. But for years it's been known—from tests conducted by the gypsum industry—that nail pops are the result of wood shrinkage. The nailhead does not loosen and pop out. Instead, the wood shrinks away from whatever is nailed to it, and the nailhead stays in place. To avoid nail pops, keep in mind that wet lumber shrinks a great deal more than dry lumber. So let lumber dry out before you begin to nail or screw it together. This is especially important when you are building with pressure-treated lumber, which usually has a high moisture content.

Also keep in mind that the amount of movement on the fastener head will be directly proportional to the length of the nail, which means the distance the nail penetrates the wood. If the nail penetrates half the thickness or width of the framing, for example, the degree of pop at the head will be equal to the shrinkage in half that framing member. That is why the industry developed shorter screws to replace nails in wallboard. The screw has the same holding power as the nail, but much less penetration.

Another industry development that has helped reduce nail pops is today's wide range of construction adhesives. When you use these adhesives, you reduce the number of nails or screws needed: Less nails equal less pops.

 Priming New Wallboard

Painting newly finished wallboard can present a challenge for the amateur because you are actually painting two materials: the paper covering on the wallboard and the compound that was used to cover nail- or screwheads, seams and corners. The paper face has a slightly rough surface, while the taping compound is glass-smooth. These two surfaces also present unequal absorption rates, and will soak up paint or primer unequally.

Because of these problems, wallboard manufacturers always advise that you use a latex or water-based primer as a first coat on new wallboard. Oil primers dry slowly, soak into the paper face of the panels, and cause the paper nap to raise. And they often cause very smooth spots where there is compound—over seams or fasteners—and very rough areas where the nap of the paper has been raised. Thus, all wallboard manufacturers recommend a heavy-bodied latex paint as a first coat over new wallboard.

One major manufacturer, United States Gypsum, makes a special base coat for new wallboard, appropriately called First Coat. It is available premixed, or you can buy the primer in powder form and mix it with water. It is cheaper than ordinary primer, and will provide the coverage of primers and sealers—without the disadvantages of either. First Coat

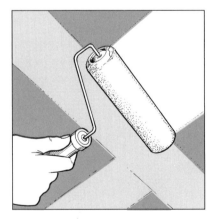

Use latex primers on newly finished drywall. Oil primers can't conceal the texture difference between the joints and surface.

will seal the surface and contains enough fillers to act as a primer, so it equalizes the absorption rate.

The Gypsum Association advises professionals to shear-coat the entire surface of the wall and ceiling with compound, so no bare paper is left. In effect, one just plasters the entire surface with taping compound, so there is no difference in texture or absorption. However, troweling a complete room can be a messy job if you are not skilled with a trowel, so we advise using First Coat as a wallboard undercoater. Once the surface differences have been eliminated with First Coat, you can then recoat with any type of paint finish.

82 Hollow-Wall Hangers

If you've ever tried to hang a rack or picture on a wall, you know there are only certain spots that hold a screw or nail—right over the studs that support the wall. Anywhere else requires a special fastener that grips the wallboard rather than the framing underneath. You'll find many types of hollow-wall fasteners at your hardware store. Most utilize a clamping mechanism that locks the unit to the wall and a screw for securing whatever it is you'd like to hang.

One type of fastener is called a Wall Grabber. Unlike some other designs, this fastener can be installed with only a hammer and screwdriver—no drill is required. And, if you ever decide to remove the fastener, you simply take out the screw, pull the base from the wall, and fill the remaining small hole with patching compound.

To install a Wall Grabber, first mark its location on the wall. Then use a hammer to drive the pointed end of the base through the wallboard. Drive the base in until it's flush with the wallboard surface, insert the screw and tighten it. As the screw is driven, it spreads the two spring-steel legs of the fastener's base. The legs lock the fastener by tightly gripping against the back of the wallboard.

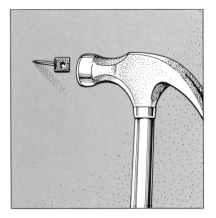

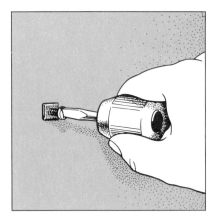

Place the pointed tip of the Wall Grabber against the wall. Then drive the fastener in until it's flush with the surface.

Use a slot-head screwdriver to drive the fastener's screw into the base. Turn the screw clockwise until it's tight.

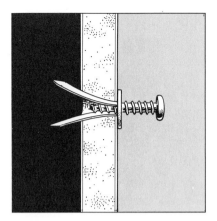 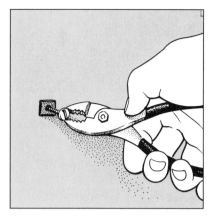

Section view of the unit shows how the two spring-steel legs of the unit spread to grip the back of the wallboard.

To remove the hanger, first back off the screw to close the steel legs. Then use pliers to pull the hanger from the wall.

83 Concrete Retaining Wall Fix

If you have a retaining wall made of concrete block, you can improve its appearance with a coat of stucco. If the block is new and clean, you can trowel on the stucco right away. Otherwise, apply a coat of concrete bonder to the wall first. Your local concrete products dealer can recommend the best bonding agent.

If the wall is badly cracked, but still standing straight, apply a layer of wire lath over the entire wall to tie the blocks together, and ensure that the stucco will adhere.

Secure the wire lath with concrete nails driven into holes bored with a masonry bit. Be sure to space the nails about 12 inches apart.

Mix a stucco base coat of one part portland cement, one part mason's cement, and two parts fine sand. Trowel this coat on to a thickness of about ½ inch, or enough to cover the wire lath if you're using it. With the base coat dry, trowel on a coat of stucco mix. After applying the first cover stucco coat, use a trowel or rubber float to create a textured-stucco pattern.

If the concrete block wall is dirty or old, apply a coat of concrete bonder before applying the stucco base coat.

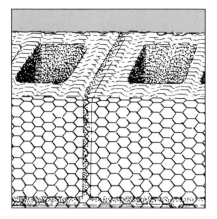

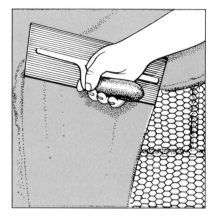

For damaged but straight concrete block walls, attach a layer of wire lath using concrete nails driven into bored holes.

Trowel base stucco coat over entire wall. Let base coat set, then apply one or more finish coats of stucco mix.

84 Painting a Textured Ceiling

For better or worse, the spray-textured ceiling became the most popular ceiling finish about 30 years ago, and in some areas it's still going strong. Its great advantage is that it reduces the time it takes to finish a ceiling properly. It also can hide defects.

The early texture materials were odd blends of taping compounds—perlite or vermiculite and whiteners—all mixed with water. The resulting textured finish was a superporous material that absorbed paint unevenly. It was this porosity and unequal paint absorption that made textured ceilings difficult to paint when they became soiled.

All spray-textured finishes are, even today, mill mixes. This means they are a combination of powdered ingredients mixed with water. Painting such finishes is almost like painting a sponge because of their heavy and unequal paint absorption. The result is that if you apply ordinary latex or oil paint, you will see roller marks or lap marks where the paint lies unevenly on the finish. To overcome this, you must apply a good sealer. Use an alkyd (oil) sealer, and apply it with a long-nap roller. The long nap reaches into the valleys in the textured pattern and ensures complete coverage.

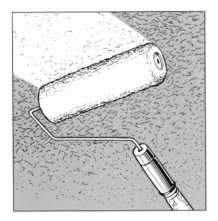

Textured surfaces, like ceilings, generally absorb paint unevenly. To prevent this, roll on an alkyd primer before painting.

Before you start the actual painting of your ceiling, the easiest way to proceed is to cover the entire floor with a canvas cloth or tarp. These are available at your local paint store. Also, buy a roller with an extension handle to apply the sealer and paint. Working with the pan on the floor and a 4-foot extension handle on the roller is a great way to prevent back strain, and it reduces the uneasiness that many people feel when on stepladders.

Apply a generous coat of sealer, checking the ceiling from several angles. Sighting from various angles will help you detect any missed spots in your sealer or paint coats.

 85 Sealing Concrete

Most homeowners are aware that exterior concrete slabs, such as driveways and patios, require a coat of sealer to protect the concrete from freezing rain, oil stains, and rust. However, even interior concrete slabs should be sealed annually to stop concrete dusting, resist stains from spills, and make cleaning easier. As an added bonus, you'll find your home is cleaner because concrete dust won't be tracked through the house.

Concrete sealer is also recommended for garage floors. Dripping road chemicals in winter can ruin concrete, and auto liquids such as oil and transmission fluid can cause stains that are nearly impossible to remove.

To seal your floor, begin by cleaning it with a concrete driveway cleaner, available from auto parts stores. Or wash the floor with TSP (trisodium phosphate) in a strong solution. When the floor is dry, apply one or two coats of concrete sealer. If you have no experience with these products, ask your local hardware store salesperson to recommend one. A paint roller, fitted with an extension handle, provides quick and easy sealer application.

Unsealed concrete floors are dusty and stain easily. To seal them, first clean the surface, then apply the sealer using a paint roller.

86 Scribing Parts to Fit

When doing home carpentry, you may face difficult fitting jobs. The method for establishing cutlines to fit uneven surfaces is called scribing. Shown in the illustration is how to scribe the back edge of a cabinet to fit against a baseboard molding. Other jobs where scribing can be used are fitting a mantel against a stone or brick fireplace, fitting a wood beam against an uneven ceiling, or fitting paneling or countertops against wavy plaster walls.

To scribe an edge to fit against any uneven surface, temporarily hold the material to be fitted into place. Measure the distance—in several places—between the uneven surface and the edge that will be cut, and note the maximum distance. Spread the compass legs to match or slightly exceed this maximum distance. Then position the metal point on one leg against the uneven surface that must be matched, and place the pencil leg on the material to be marked.

Now slide the compass along the uneven material so its shape is recorded on the material to be cut. Remove any temporary clamps or nails, and use a band saw or saber saw to cut along the uneven scribe line. After cutting along the scribe line, you should have a perfect fit where the material abuts the uneven wall or other surface.

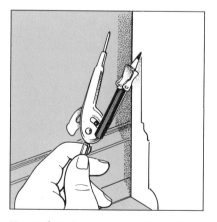

Use a drawing compass to scribe a cutline that matches an uneven surface. Move slowly and keep the point and pencil even.

87 Removing Old Flooring

A couple of common repair issues are how to remove old tile and adhesives from walls or floors, and how to remove sponge carpet pad when it's time to recarpet. Your first option is a rental machine that has a horizontal cutting knife to cut loose the old floor covering. But if your problem is vinyl tile or linoleum over a wood floor, you often can leave the old floor covering in place. Simply cover it with a layer of ³⁄₁₆-inch-thick lauan plywood. Then install your new flooring over this new plywood. This is much easier than tearing up the old floor covering and fighting to remove the old adhesive. Laying plywood over the old floor is especially recommended if the old floor covering contains asbestos.

If you must remove the old adhesive or rubber carpet backing, use a scraper with a razor edge. You can also soften these adhesives for removal by using a commercial adhesive remover available at floor tile dealers. These products soften adhesives used on plastic and ceramic tile, cove base or any all-purpose latex adhesive, including that used with foam-backed carpet. They're also great for simply removing adhesives from the surface of wall tiles or flooring. Let the remover set a few minutes and scrape away the adhesive with a putty knife or paint scraper. Some of these products do contain methylene chloride, so be sure to supply adequate ventilation to the area.

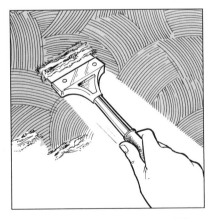

A simple wallpaper scraper with a razor blade does a great job removing old adhesive. Always push the tool away from you.

88 Quieting Floor Noises

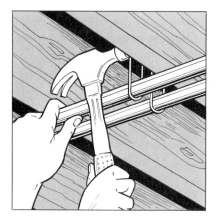

To stop the noise from pipes rubbing together, separate the pipes and reset them using hanger brackets driven into the joists.

To dampen a variety of pipe noises, install foam insulation over the pipes. The insulation will also reduce condensation.

Many times, what we call floor squeaks are only noises and have nothing to do with squeaking floors. Plumbing pipes, bridging and heating ducts can pop and crackle, and even squeak, when we walk or roll something across the floor.

The easiest way to find the source of any noise is to have someone walk across the floor while you listen carefully below. Noises that seem to come from heating duct locations can be traced down and eliminated by loosening brackets that connect the ducts to the underside of floor joists. Sometimes a piece of rubber material, such as weather stripping, can be wedged between the air duct and the joists to provide a sort of shock absorber between the two.

You should also check pipe locations where V-shaped pipe hangers support water or gas pipes. Joists that flex when they're walked on can rub against pipes and create a noise. Adjust the pipe hangers to relieve the rubbing.

Pipes can also make noises when they expand from hot water, contract from cold water, or vibrate or *hammer* from high pressure. Foam pipe insulation can be used to cushion the pipe and muffle expansion or pressure noises. The insulation will also help prevent condensation from forming on the pipes which can cause water puddles on basement floors.

153

89 Installing Carpet.

Much of today's carpeting is made of man-made fiber that's held together by a latex or foam backing. When it's new, carpet is very stiff and difficult to handle. But a few easy installation tips will help you add flexibility to the carpet so it will easily fit into odd shapes and around stair steps.

If at all possible, lay the carpet flat, unrolled, to let it relax and lose any wrinkles that resulted from rolling. If you have a large paved area, such as a driveway or patio, unroll the carpet outdoors, so the sun can warm and soften the backing. This will make the carpet more flexible.

If you are working in cold or wet weather, unroll the carpet in a basement or garage and leave it open for a day or two. If you still have trouble fitting the carpet around any obstacles, apply moisture to the backing, using a common plant mister. This moisture will soften the latex backing. If the carpet is still stiff, augment the moisture treatment with heat. Use a hair dryer or heat gun to warm the backing. It will become as flexible as ordinary fabric, so you can shape it easily.

When the carpet is ready to lay, use double-faced carpet tape (it has adhesive on both sides) to hold the carpet in place. If you've let the carpet relax and lose its wrinkles, you can often install the foam-backed carpet without even using a stretcher. Of course, you can always rent carpet tools such as stretchers and hot-melt seam tools at carpet or rental outlets.

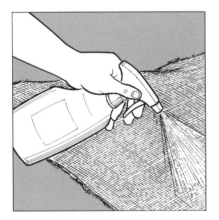

To make a stiff new carpet more flexible, dampen the backing with a plant sprayer or warm it with a heat gun or hair dryer.

90 Repairing Carpet

If you have a small stain or burn in your carpet, you can repair it with a special carpet patch cutting tool that professional carpet installers call a cookie cutter. This tool cuts away the damaged area and cuts a matching plug to fill the hole. You can buy the tool and adhesive disks for securing the patch at carpet supply dealers.

The cutter has a pair of razor blades at its perimeter. Just position the cutter over the damaged area of the carpet, press gently and turn. When the damaged section is removed, peel the face off the adhesive-backed disk. Insert the disk into the hole so it's centered and laps under the hole perimeter uniformly. Press the carpet to secure it to the disk. Then, use the cutter to make a repair plug from a piece of scrap carpet or from a section of the carpet that's hidden, such as inside a closet. Press the plug in place so it sticks to the disk. If the edges don't quite match, lift the plug, coat the edges with carpet adhesive and replace the plug. You can further blend the patch by running a vacuum cleaner over the area, or by using a comb to blend the carpet fibers together.

To remove a small damaged area of carpet, use a carpet repair cutter. Press cutter gently and turn until cut is completed.

155

Peel off back of adhesive disk and insert into hole, adhesive side up. Center disk and press carpet around hole to secure disk.

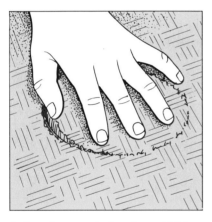

Cut replacement plug from hidden carpet and press plug into hole. Brush surface to blend fibers together.

CHAPTER EIGHT

101

ELECTRICITY

TIPS

91 Yard Light Maintenance

A yard light can keep silent watch in your yard, revealing intruders, welcoming guests, and even preventing tripping or falling injuries. So to keep these lights in good repair and working properly, give them about a half-hour of attention each year.

The first step is to repaint the light post. This is a simple procedure of lightly sanding the post and applying the fresh paint. If you mask any outlets or the electronic eye on the post, you can quickly paint, using a sponge brush or aerosol can.

While you have the light globe removed, and with the current turned off, clean the light socket to remove any corrosion. With the light exposed to all kinds of weather, moisture often reaches the socket and causes some corrosion. To clean the contacts, use an emery board, the sort that smooths fingernails. The boards are abrasive enough to clean the socket, but are not so hard as to cause damage.

Once the socket is clean, blow away any bits of corrosion, then give the socket a protective shot of silicone ignition sealer. This helps seal the socket against corrosion and moisture, and it lubricates the socket so the light bulb is easy to install and to remove when it needs to be replaced.

To maintain yard lights, first shut off power and remove globe and bulb. Clean away erosion in the socket with an emery board.

After the socket is clean, blow away any dirt. Then spray auto ignition sealer into the socket and replace the bulb and globe.

92 Installing a Fan Control

When you start shopping for a ceiling fan, you may find that a variable-speed feature costs a lot more than single-speed models. Keep in mind that you can make any ceiling fan variable speed by installing an adjustable fan control.

The fan control shown here is a rheostat type, with a switch handle that slides up and down. Similar controls are available as light dimmer switches. But these switches are not intended to control fan motors and are not equal to the task. Fan control switches should have at least a 5-amp capacity.

To install the fan control (we are assuming the fan is connected to a ceiling light box), shut off the electric power to the circuit, then remove the old switch from the box. Straighten out the ends of the electrical wires in the box. Then join the pigtail wires from the back of the fan control to the ends of the box wires. Join the white wires together and the black wires together using the proper-sized Wire-Nuts. Replace the switch cover, turn on the power, and test the control to make sure that your fan is working properly.

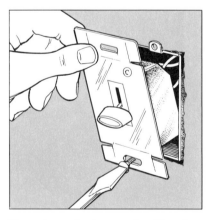

To make a single-speed ceiling fan into a variable-speed model, just replace your wall switch with a variable-speed fan control.

93 Wiring Connections

If you've tried connecting two electrical wires together with Wire-Nuts, you may have had trouble getting the Wire-Nuts to hold. The trouble may be that you first twisted the wires together. When the nut would not tighten, you may have tried holding it in place with electrician's tape, and ended with a messy and bulky connection.

To join two wires together, strip the insulation back about ¾ inch from the wire ends. Hold the two wires alongside—and parallel to—each other. Slip the Wire-Nut over the ends of the wires and tighten it. Then tug on each wire to test the connection. Do not add electrician's tape: The Wire-Nut will stay firmly in place.

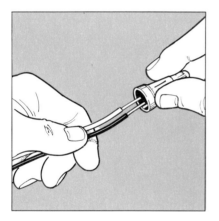

When joining wires, do not twist them around each other. Leave them straight and simply turn the Wire-Nut onto the ends.

 94 Wiring Outlets

Have you ever removed an electrical outlet and noted the clean attachment of the wire to the outlet screw? Electricians have a secret for making those neat connections on new work.

First, leave the wires long in outlet boxes you are wiring—don't cut them so short you have no wire to work with. When you are ready to attach the receptacle or outlet, cut the wires about 8 inches long and use a wire stripper to remove the insulation about 2 inches from the end. Don't use a knife to strip the insulation. A knife may nick the wires and cause them to break when they are flexed.

Now wrap the wire around the proper receptacle screw (white wire to silver screw, black wire to brass screw) in a clockwise direction. Tighten the screw. Now grasp the end of the wire and bend it back and forth until it breaks off. You now have a professional-looking connection between the wires and the receptacle.

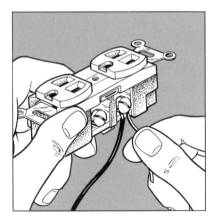

To make wire connections like a pro, wrap the stripped wire end around the screw, tighten the screw, and break off the wire.

95 Installing a Motion Detector Light

It is a shocking experience to return home to find that your home has been burglarized and your prize possessions stolen in your absence. It is even more traumatic to awaken from a sound sleep to hear sounds of someone forcing an entry into your home. While it is not pleasant to dwell on thoughts of increased security needs, statistics tell us that one out of four homes in the United States will be burglarized this year. One possible solution is to have sophisticated—and expensive—electronic security alarms installed in your home. But in most residential areas one can discourage all but the most persistent professional burglars with a few low-cost devices that the homeowner can install himself.

One such security device is the infrared motion-detector light that senses a change in temperature from the movement of people, cars, or other moving objects, and turns on bright floodlights to welcome guests or warn of intruders. The lights can be installed near likely entry points such as back and front doors, and can also provide security for family members returning home after dark.

The light fixture installed here has sensors that detect movement within an arc that is 60 feet wide and 60 feet long. There is a sensitivity (SENS) control that adjusts the amount of heat required to activate the control module and turn on the lights. Another control is a built-in photo-cell (DAYLIGHT) that prevents the light from turning on in daylight: You can adjust the setting to permit the lights to come on at the desired level of darkness. A third (TIME) control lets you decide how long the lights will stay on when triggered. (Ours ranges from 15 seconds to 18 minutes.)

The motion detector light kits are available at home centers or lighting dealers, with prices starting at an affordable $25, a price that includes both the fixture and flood lights not included in the kit.

Installation of the light is quite easy: proceed as you would to install any exterior light fixture. Turn off the power to the light by removing the fuses or turning off the breaker switches at the electric entry service box. Remove the old fixture and connect the motion detector wires to the service wires from the electrical box. The black wire in the box is the power wire: Connect the red wire from the motion sensor to the black wire from the box, the white sensor wire to the white wire in the box, and the green or ground wire to the green wire in the box. Switch on the power and test the light.

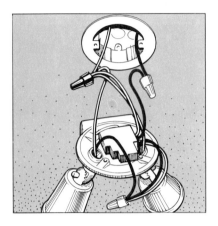

Turn off electric power to light. Remove the old fixture and install the motion sensor fixture. Use Wire-Nuts to attach the fixture wires: black or red wires to the black (power) wire from the outlet box, white wire to white (neutral) wire in the outlet box, and green to green (ground) wire in the outlet box.

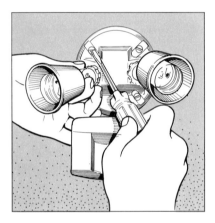

Carefully fold all wires behind the motion detector and use screws to secure the new fixture to the outlet box. Turn on power and test the light.

96 Installing a GFCI Receptacle

Each electrical circuit in your home is equipped with a fuse or circuit breaker that is designed to protect that circuit from fire in case of a short circuit or equipment breakdown on the circuit. However, fuses and circuit breakers will not act quickly enough to prevent dangerous or fatal electrical shock to humans, so the electrical codes decree that some outlets must be fitted with ground fault circuit interrupters, or GFCIs. They are most important in any area where the person may come in contact with moisture or water: Outlets in the kitchen, bathroom and laundry, plus exterior outlets, must be equipped with these safety devices.

In an electric circuit, the black or power wire carries the current to the fixture or outlet, and an equal current returns to the service panel via the white or neutral wire. The GFCI is a device that measures the equal flow of current both incoming (on the black wire) and returning (on the white wire). However, if any current goes to ground, as would happen if a person in contact with the current began to experience a shock, the GFCI senses the difference in current between the hot or black wire and the neutral or white wire, and shuts down the current before it can harm a person. A GFCI will sense a difference in current of as little as 5 milliamps, and will shut down the current before injury to the person can occur.

Note that you should always turn off the power at the service panel before working on any electrical circuit. Note also that there may be a

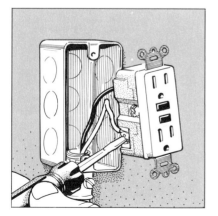

A GFCI designed to protect a single outlet is installed just like any electrical outlet. Turn off the power to the outlet, disconnect the existing outlet, and install the new GFCI. Attach the black wire to the brass screw and the white wire to the silver screw. Turn on the power, push the set button, and check the outlet.

difference between GFCIs: Be sure to buy the proper GFCI for your application and install it according to directions. Some GFCIs have two pairs of white and black wires, and can be installed on the electrical outlet box nearest the service panel to protect the entire circuit downstream. The GFCI shown here was installed in a laundry room, and protects only the electrical outlet that serves the washing machine and dryer.

97 Installing On-Wall Wiring

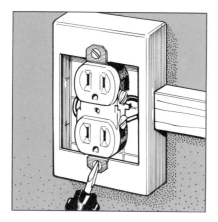

Wiring is attached to the source or existing outlet: black (power) wire to brass screw, white (neutral) wire to silver screw, and green (ground) wire to green screw. The plastic channel is cut for length and screwed to the wall or ceiling. Then a new baseplate is screwed to the surface at the new outlet location, and the new outlet is attached to the wiring.

A box or outlet extension fits atop the base outlet plate. The extension provides depth to the outlet box so there is room to conceal the wiring and mount the new outlet.

Would you like to have an extra electrical outlet on a wall or ceiling, but feel you don't have the expertise to string electrical wiring through finished partitions? Consider installing an on-wall wiring system such as Wiremold. These wiring systems use a system of plastic baseplates and outlet extension boxes to increase the depth of existing outlet boxes so you can install extra wiring. To install on-wall wiring, a baseplate and extension box are installed at a source outlet. Then the base portion of a plastic wire channel is cut to length to reach to the desired new outlet location and is installed using #6 pan head screws to attach the wire channel to the wall or ceiling. At the new box location a baseplate unit is screwed to the surface. Wiring is run through the wire channel and a new receptacle is attached to the wires (black wires to brass screws, white wires to silver screws, green wires to green screws). Install a box extension on the new baseplate and screw the new receptacle to the extension and baseplate. Finally, screw the cover plates back on the existing and new outlet boxes and turn on the power.

98 Replacing a Lamp Holder

Pull-chain lamp holders are used to provide lighting or a power source at a point that is not served by a switch. The lamp holder may have a single lamp (bulb) socket or may also have an outlet to accept a cord plug. Because they eliminate the use of a switch, pull-chain lamp holders are basically used for economy and are often found in unfinished basements, garages, attics, and storage spaces. With repeated use, the pull-chain switch may fail and you'll have to replace the lamp holder.

Turn off the power at the fuse or circuit breaker on the circuit that supplies power to the lamp holder. Remove the bulb from the socket, then remove the two screws that secure the lamp-holder base to the outlet box. Unscrew the assembly ring and base to gain access to the switch mechanism. You will find two terminal screws on the switch mechanism, with a black (power) wire attached to one screw terminal and a white (neutral) wire attached to the other terminal screw. Loosen both terminal screws and remove the electrical wires from the failed switch.

Attach the new switch mechanism to the two wires, making sure that the terminal screws are tightly secured. Then slip the pull-chain end

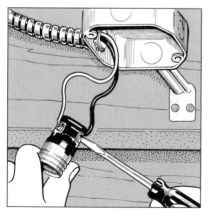

Remove the old lamp holder as per text. Attach the new switch mechanism, securing the black and white wires to the two screw terminals.

through the chain hole and push the switch mechanism into the lamp-holder base. Turn the assembly ring threads onto the threaded base of the switch mechanism and tighten it. Then use the two retaining screws to attach the lamp-holder base to the outlet box. Turn on the electricity and pull the switch chain to test the new lamp holder.

The lamp holder consists of three pieces: the switch mechanism, the base, and the assembly ring. You must unscrew the assembly ring to gain access to the switch terminals.

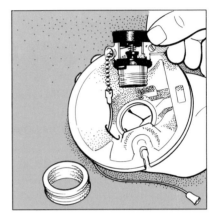

To assemble the lamp holder, pull the switch chain through the chain hole, slip the switch mechanism into the hole in the base, and screw the assembly ring onto the threaded base of the switch mechanism.

99 Using Circuit and Continuity Testers

For safety when working on electrical circuits, one should always be sure that the power is turned off. The easy way to check for power is to learn to use an inexpensive circuit tester. A circuit tester is a device that has a base containing a neon light and two probes used to complete an electric circuit. The tester can be used to test for power at a switch, outlet, fuse, or electrical cord. The tester also can find short circuits, check circuit polarity, and test motors or appliances.

To check for power at a receptacle, insert the two metal probes into the wide (neutral) and narrow (hot) slots. If the neon bulb glows, there is power at the receptacle; if the bulb does not glow, the power is off and the receptacle is safe to work on. To check the receptacle for ground, insert one probe into the narrow (hot) slot and the other into the lower or U-shaped hole. The neon light should glow. Then insert one probe into the wide (neutral) slot and the other into the U-shaped ground hole. The neon light should not glow.

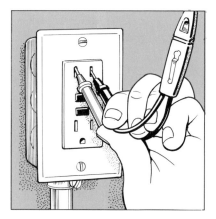

To be sure power is off, insert one probe of a circuit tester into the narrow (hot) slot, the other probe into the wide (neutral) slot. If the neon light does not glow, power is off and it should be safe to work on the receptacle.

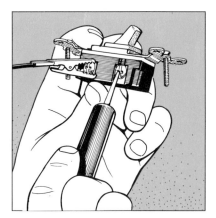

To test an electrical switch, turn the switch on. Place the alligator clip on one screw and the probe point on the other screw. If the tester bulb lights the switch is working. If the bulb does not light, replace the switch.

A continuity tester is used to check circuits, cords, and switches for continuity. The testing is done with the power off. The unit shown uses a pair of AAA batteries to supply the test power. There are two probes: a nail-shaped probe on the end of the tester body and an alligator clip connected to the body with an electrical wire.

To test an extension cord for continuity, attach the alligator clip to one of the cord prongs: In the illustration we are testing the ground. Insert the metal probe into the U-shaped ground hole in the socket end of the cord. If the tester's bulb lights, the ground wire is intact or continuous. In the same way we can test the hot and neutral wires in the cord.

To test a light switch, be sure the switch is in the "on" position. Attach the alligator clip to one screw terminal on the switch and the metal probe to the other screw terminal. If the switch is working, the bulb will light.

To test an extension cord, attach the alligator clip to the cord prong, and insert the probe into the corresponding slot at the other end of the cord. If the wire being tested (ground wire test shown) is continuous, the tester bulb will glow. If a test of any pair of slots and prongs fails, there is a break in the cord.

100 Removing a Broken Light Bulb

Suppose you drop a lamp or work light and the glass bulb breaks down to the socket. How can you get the broken bulb base out of the socket?

The first step is to disconnect the lamp or work light, or turn off the power at the fuse or circuit breaker if the broken bulb is in a fixed light fixture. Don't touch the open filament on the light bulb until you are certain the power is off. If you have a pair of needle-nose pliers handy, just slip the tip of the pliers into the socket, grasp the base of the light bulb, and screw it out of the socket. If you don't have a pair of needle-nose pliers handy, try this trick for the non-handy: Press the end of a bar of hand soap into the broken base, being careful not to cut your hands. Then twist the bar of soap slowly to unscrew the bulb base from the socket.

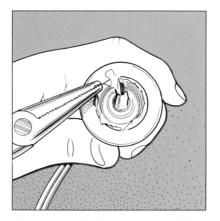

Disconnect the lamp or turn off the power to the light fixture. Then use needle-nose pliers to grasp the base of the broken bulb and twist it loose. Otherwise, press the end of a bar of soap into the bulb's base and twist.

101 Refrigerator Maintenance

Modern refrigerators require little maintenance, but to keep your appliance in peak operating condition and to cut down on electricity consumption, there are a few maintenance chores that should not be overlooked.

The first step is to keep the exposed coil on the back of the refrigerator clean and free of dust and lint. Dirt and dust that accumulates on the coils will make the machine work harder to cool the refrigerator interior. At least twice per year, use a clean paintbrush or a hand vacuum cleaner to clean dust from the coils at the back of the appliance.

Check also at the bottom of the refrigerator for a condensate tray. This tray catches small amounts of water when the refrigerator self-defrosts. If neglected, the condensate tray can develop mold growth that can be a hazard to those with respiratory problems. The condensate tray is concealed behind the base trim on the bottom front of the refrigerator. Slide the condensate tray forward to remove it. It should be washed four times per year or as outlined in your owner's manual.

To check the weather stripping on your refrigerator door, position a dollar bill in the door and shut it. Pull gently on the dollar bill to see if the weather stripping is worn. If the dollar bill slips easily out of the door, replace the weather stripping.

Position a dollar bill in the refrigerator door and shut the door. If the weather stripping is good, the dollar bill will be hard to withdraw.

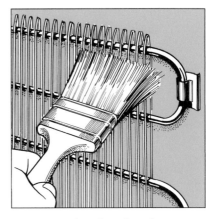

Remove and clean the condensate tray at the bottom of the refrigerator.

Use a paintbrush or hand vacuum to clean the coils at the back of the refrigerator.

CHAPTER NINE

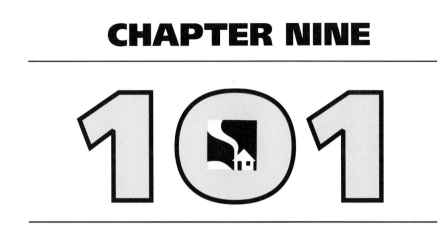

TOOLS

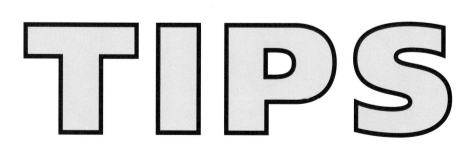

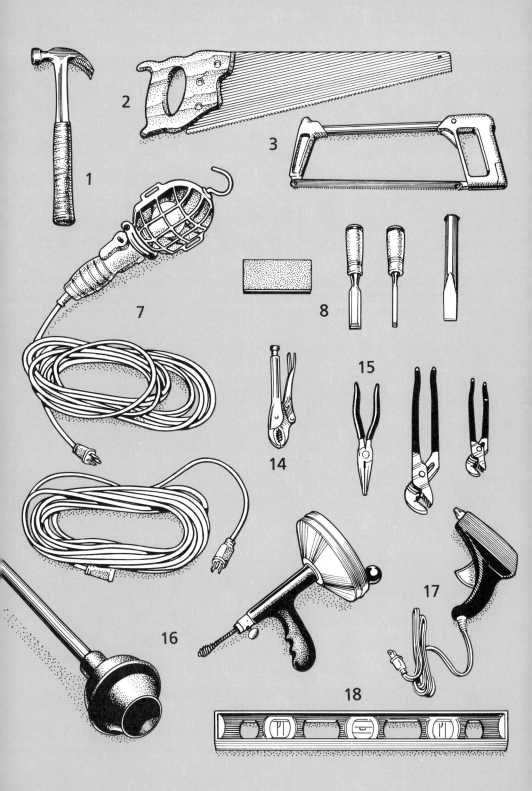

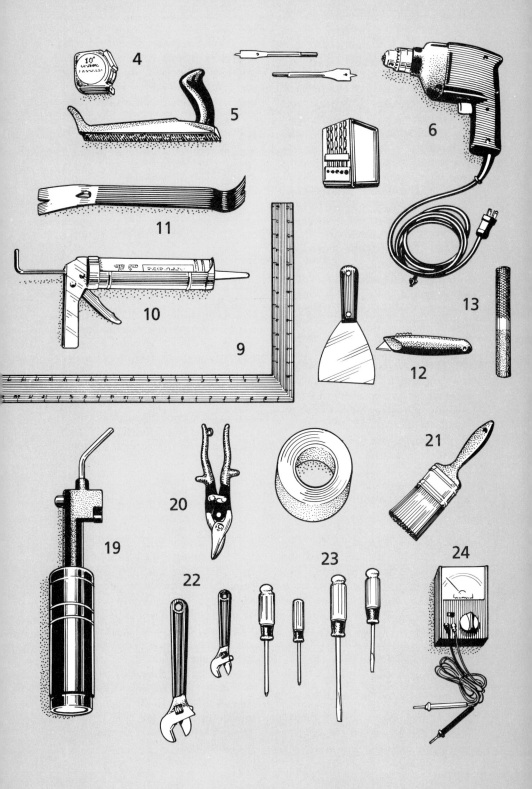

Moving into a new home may seem like a ticket to trouble-free living, but that's not always the case. A new home is like a new car, it sometimes takes a while to work the bugs out. And in the arena of the lowest bidder, even a custom home will harbor a few blemishes and oversights. Then too, neither you nor your builder will foresee all the minor changes and upgrades you'll want after moving in. When the construction dust settles, chances are you'll still need a few tools.

With reasonable care most quality tools will last a lifetime. To ensure that this happens, follow a few simple guidelines when working:

Always use a tool for the job it was designed for, and never use a tool that you want to keep in good shape for a project that may bend, dull, or otherwise impair its ability to work the way it should. When using tools around water, always dry them after the job is completed or at the end of the day. Apply a light coating of oil to metal tool parts with a rag. Remove any rust by rubbing the affected area with a piece of steel wool dipped in a solvent such as kerosene. Remove sawdust from motor vents on power tools.

You may not need or want all the tools we've compiled for the ideal home tool kit, but you'll probably find the need for most at one time or another. You might buy the basics now and add the specialty tools later when you need them. In any case, here's our selection, along with a few words on each tool's features and most likely uses.

(1) CLAW HAMMER

A good finishing hammer will last a lifetime and help you through a wide variety of improvement and repair projects. A hammer with a steel or fiberglass handle will be the most durable, especially when pulling nails. We suggest one with a curved claw and a 1-pound head. This combination will work well on rough carpentry as well as finish work. A quality hammer, in the $16 to $20 range, can mean the difference between driving nails and bending them.

(2) HANDSAW

Next on your list will be a good crosscut saw. Handsaws cost a good deal less ($10 to $16) than powered saws and work just as well in limited-use situations. You'll also be able to reach into spaces too cramped for a circular saw. A 10-point crosscut saw, having ten teeth points per inch, will serve you well around the house and yard. This saw will cut clean enough for most finish work and quickly enough for most rough work. If you'll be doing mostly rough carpentry, a 6- or 8-point saw will speed your work greatly.

(3) HACKSAW

There are many occasions when a hacksaw comes in handy, from cutting plumbing pipes to trimming downspouts and slicing through ceramic tile. The most important thing to look for is rigidity. A saw that flexes when used will bend or break the blade, or will simply refuse to cut straight. Most are adjustable and will accept 10- or 12-inch blades. Look for a brand that provides for two different blade installations, either straight or at a 45° angle. A good quality hacksaw will cost between $12 and $16, a nominal fee for a very useful tool.

(4) TAPE MEASURE

The best advice we can give in selecting a tape measure is to avoid the short and narrow. For general household use, choose one that is at least ¾ inch wide and 15 feet long, and clips to a belt or pocket. Beyond that, it's a matter of which style appeals to you most. And remember, a broken tape does not always mean a ruined tape measure. Replacement tapes are available for most brands. We chose a tape measure costing only $11, even though cheaper ones are available.

(5) PLANE

For trimming marginal thicknesses of lumber, consider buying a plane. As planes require exact adjustment and dull easily when used by untrained hands, a Surform-type tool is a good household alternative. This type of plane has a replaceable, slotted blade that gouges out narrow ribbons of wood, plastic, vinyl, and even aluminum, all without clogging. Unlike other planes, it will not yield the clean, hard-edged surface of a block plane, but it's a snap to use. We paid just under $12 for a 10-inch model.

(6) ⅜-INCH DRILL

Another tool that will quickly earn its keep is a ⅜-inch drill. While cordless drills are ideal for the quick fix, a cord-type drill is more versatile. And because you won't be paying for a charger, you'll get more power per dollar invested. Look for one with a variable-speed, reversible motor capable of at least 2000 RPMs. The one we chose has 2.8 amps of power and offers an industry-standard 1-year warranty. We paid just under $70.

You'll also want a selection of drill bits and possibly a few specialty attachments. We chose a 13-piece, high-speed bit set with sizes graduating from ⅟₁₆ to ¼ inch. Buying bits in a case makes selection easier and also reveals at a glance which sizes you'll need to replace.

In addition to the $16 set, we chose ½- and ¾-inch spade bits designed for boring larger holes in wood. Spade bits are reasonably priced, around $2.50 each, and are easily resharpened. A ⅜-inch drill also accepts a variety of bits and attachments such as a magnetized nut driver which drives self-tapping sheet-metal screws.

(7) EXTENSION CORDS AND TROUBLE LIGHTS

To keep your projects well powered and better lighted, you'll need a grounded extension cord and a trouble light. A drop cord in the 30- to 50-foot category will serve most needs, but don't skimp on its wire size. A lightweight cord will allow too much voltage drop, which will in turn shorten the life of the tool or appliance it serves. Generally speaking, the longer the cord the heavier it will need to be.

We chose a grounded 30-foot model with 16-gauge wire and a carrying capacity of 13 amps, which was priced at about $10.

As for trouble lights, look for the same features. If the light you fancy does not have a receptacle, an ungrounded cord will do. We paid just under $11 for a 25-foot model with a plastic cage.

(8) CHISELS AND A SHARPENING STONE

Every household should have a chisel or two for roughing out of wood or drywall that can't be reached with a larger, more precise tool. And as many of us can blunt the edges of chisels just by picking them up, you'll also want a double-sided (fine/course) sharpening stone. When used with honing oil, a sharpening stone will resharpen the edges of all but the most abused chisels and knives.

You'll need to decide which sizes best suit your purposes, but two will often do. We chose ¼- and ¾-inch chisels and a 5 × 2-inch combination stone. We paid $6 and $8 for the chisels and $12 for the sharpening stone.

And finally, you may want a cold chisel in your toolbox for those materials not made of wood. A cold chisel can be used to chip concrete or split light-gauge metal. It's especially handy for cutting bricks, blocks, and paving stones. We paid $6 for a hefty 1-inch model.

(9) FRAMING SQUARE

A framing square in the hands of a professional can work wonders, but even a beginner will find this a useful tool, if only as straightedge and angle finder. It can be used to check the squareness of a room before laying floor coverings or to ensure a square cut in plywood or dimensional lumber. You'll find them in steel and aluminum for around $10.

(10) CAULK GUN

With everything from caulk and glue to grout and roofing tar packaged in tubes these days, a good caulk gun is a must. Expect to find two or three levels of quality in caulk guns. Go right past the bargain basket on your way to those in the $4 to $5 range. These mid-priced guns will accom-

modate all ⅒-gallon tubes and are sturdy enough for years of casual use.

(11) PRY BAR

A pry bar is another useful tool, with more real-life uses than its manufacturers probably intended. A pry bar is designed to pry things apart, primarily pieces of wood. It is equipped with beveled nail claws at each end and has a curved shank ending in a sharp right angle. When a block of wood is placed under one end, it makes a great lever and fulcrum. Invest $8 or $9 in one of these and you're just about guaranteed that you'll find a way to use it.

(12) KNIVES

Everyone is familiar with the uses of a putty knife, but when you head out to buy one, consider upsizing to a 4-inch drywall knife for greater versatility. A flexible drywall knife can be used to apply spackling, scrape paint, strip furniture, or press wallpaper into corners. Make sure that the model you choose has a chrome-plated blade to resist corrosive drywall compounds. Beyond that, the choice is yours. We paid $8 for ours.

You'll also want a sturdy utility knife for cutting open cartons, trimming wallpaper and floor coverings, and for a dozen other chores. We suggest a knife with a retractable blade for easier and safer storage. You'll find plenty of good utility knives in the $5 to $7 category.

(13) FOUR-IN-ONE RASP/FILE

You might also consider purchasing a combination wood rasp and file for your tool kit. With both a course and fine rasp, as well as a course and fine file on each tool, you'll be able to shape wood and sharpen garden tools whenever the need arises, and for under $9.

(14) LOCKING PLIERS

Locking pliers first became popular in shipyards during World War II. Before long they found their way into just about every mechanic's toolbox and have lately turned up in a good many kitchen drawers as well. This tool is so popular because it can do so much. It's a plier, a makeshift wrench, a wire cutter, and a sturdy clamp, which is about all you can ask of a tool costing between $10 and $12.

(15) SLIP-JAW AND NEEDLE-NOSE PLIERS

Slip-jaw pliers make a good choice because the jaws are able to expand to meet the job requirements. Their offset jaw configuration also provides a little more leverage than standard pliers. We decided on two sizes, a 6½- and a 10-inch model. The smaller pliers are good for small household projects, while the larger version will easily handle the chrome or plastic trap nuts on plumbing fixtures. With new home construction including almost all plastic pipes and fittings, this size makes a good substitute for a standard pipe wrench. We paid $9 for the smaller pliers and $11 for the larger ones. The 8-inch needle-nose pliers shown here have a long reach for getting into cramped spaces, which is where needle-nose pliers work best. This one also has a wire cutter built into the jaws. Expect good needle-nose pliers to cost between $8 and $9.

(16) DRAIN AUGER AND PLUNGER

There's a perverse physical law that has drains clogging only when plumbers and drain services are hard to reach, and if you are lucky enough to find one that will answer your call for help quickly, the job will likely be frightfully expensive. Drain clogs like holidays best.

For those times and others, plan ahead and invest in an inexpensive drain auger. The one shown here costs a mere $15 and will work in most situations. Avoid the simple, bare-cable type augers; they won't give enough cranking power in problem situations.

A plunger is the other half of the clogged drain solution. Most clogs can be broken free with a good plunger, almost to the complete exclusion of caustic chemicals. Look for one that has a large cup with a folding funnel. With the funnel folded in, this plunger will work well on sinks and tubs. Folded out, it's perfect for toilet clogs, and all for a mere $5. Avoid purchasing smaller plungers. While they're easy to store, you'll get little clog-busting force out of them.

In addition to these tools, you may also want to include a pipe wrench to round out your plumbing tool needs and forestall other difficulties later.

(17) HOT GLUE GUN

Hot glue guns used to be hobby tools, but more and more of us are finding them useful around the house. They work especially well in repairing small fittings on toys and other household items, especially plastics. Best of all, hot glue sets as soon as it cools, which can speed things up substantially. You'll find inexpensive versions that are fed simply by pushing the glue stick through the gun. Others, such as the one shown here, feature a trigger-feed mechanism that offers better control when applying the glue. Expect to pay between $17 and $19 for a trigger-feed model.

(18) LEVEL

A good 2-foot level is another tool you'll find yourself using over and over again. It can level picture frames, start wallpaper, measure short items, level appliances, and provide a straightedge for a knife or pencil. You'll find them made of steel, aluminum, plastic, and wood. The metal versions offer the most versatility and strength for the money, which in this case was just under $14.

(19) PROPANE TORCH

When making plumbing improvements, a propane torch will put the most distance between you and a professional plumber. As a skill, soldering is largely overrated. But you will need a torch. You'll find two varieties in home centers. One will require that you light it with a striker or match. The other is self-starting. We chose the substantially more expensive model simply because the self-starting feature is so handy. Just turn it on and pull the trigger for a clean blue flame. The price of this self-starter was just under $28. Purchase a small tin of flux and a roll of lead-free solder along with the torch. (The EPA has prohibited the use of high-lead solders in plumbing since 1986.) Many torches come with soldering instructions. Read the instructions and practice with a few

fittings and some copper pipe. If you buy a self-cleaning flux, you won't even need to sand the pipe and fittings.

(20) TIN SNIPS

Tin snips may seem at the outer edge of household tool selection, but when you need them there's no substitute. Try cutting an extra heat register in an unfinished basement without them. If the need arises, choose a pair designed to cut along a straight line. They can be made to cut wide, sweeping curves as well. Our selection cost $17.

While you're at it, buy a roll of quality duct tape. You may never need it for duct-work, but you'll find a use for it just about everywhere else. Expect to pay $5 to $6 for a 2-inch roll that is 60 yards long.

(21) PAINTBRUSHES

When it comes to paintbrushes, don't skimp. Cheap throwaways have a way of finding their own revenge. The material your brush is made from should be determined by your choice of paint. A brush with polyester or nylon bristles is suitable for latex or oil paint.

If you're going to buy one brush, make it polyester. Brushes made from hog bristle are best used with oil paints and get limp when used with latex paint. Good quality bristle brushes are expensive. Don't buy inexpensive bristle brushes; they lose their bristles. For a quick touch-up, use a small, inexpensive foam brush. Don't load it with too much paint; these brushes have a habit of dripping.

Consider brush shape when you're buying supplies. Brushes are available with tapered or straight bristles. The straight cuts work best on large areas, while the tapered versions work better as trim brushes. You may need both, but a straight bristle brush is a good start.

(22) ADJUSTABLE WRENCHES

We recommend two adjustable wrenches for projects around the house and garage. A 6-inch wrench will work well in tightening furniture bolts, toilet bolts, appliance leveling legs, and the like. A 10-inch spanner will handle many plumbing repairs and do double duty in automotive work. Adjustable wrenches are available at several price levels. Avoid the low-end imports like the plague; mid-priced versions should serve you quite well for many years.

(23) SCREWDRIVERS

Screwdrivers are typically the most abused tools going. As such, steer clear of bargain-priced screwdrivers. Look for handles that are large enough to be comfortable and shanks that are long enough to let you see your work. The better brands will have hardened steel tips and may be magnetized. We recommend two Phillips-head and two slotted-head screwdrivers in small and medium sizes. The combination will cost between $10 and $12.

(24) OHMMETER

An ohmmeter is a good choice if you plan to handle your own electrical problems. With it, you'll be able to test for voltage, continuity, and ohm levels. It can be used for checking out your home's electrical system, both wiring and devices, as well as the appliances within your home. An ohmmeter will tell you if a switch is defective (by checking continuity), or if the problem lies elsewhere. Simple ohmmeters start at around $25.

In addition to an ohmmeter, you'll also want to have on hand several other tools when undertaking electrical work.

A voltage tester consists of two probes joined by a tiny neon light. It is commonly used to determine whether power is present in a set of wires or a receptacle. Also purchase a continuity tester, which will help you in testing if a switch or circuit is in operating condition. A continuity tester differs from a voltage tester in that it has a power source—a small battery. When the alligator clip at one end of the tester is touched to the probe at the other end, a circuit is completed and the light within the tester lights up in the handle. In like fashion, any device placed between the clip and probe will complete the circuit if it is in operating order.

GLOSSARY

airlock A blockage in a pipe caused by a trapped bubble of air.

alkyd paint An oil-based paint made of alkyd and other synthetic resins, slower drying but more durable than latex paint.

appliance A machine or device powered by electricity. Or a functional piece of equipment connected to the plumbing—a basin, sink, bath, etc.

batten A narrow strip of wood.

bleeder valve A valve on one side of a radiator that can be loosened to let trapped air escape from the heating system.

circuit A complete path through which an electrical current can flow.

cold patch A thick epoxy used to seal cracks in asphalt.

concave Curving inward.

conductor A component, usually a length of wire, along which an electrical current will pass.

convex Curving outward.

countersink To cut a tapered recess which allows the head of a screw to lie flush with a surface. Also the tapered recess itself.

damper A paddlelike device inside a duct that regulates airflow to different parts of a house in a forced-air system.

diazinon A pesticide with a low to moderate level of toxicity.

drain valve A spigot at the base of a water heater that releases water when opened.

drywall Prefabricated panels consisting of a gypsum core surrounded by a paper cover used for walls and ceilings in home interiors.

efflorescence A white powdery deposit caused by soluble salts migrating to the surface of masonry.

fascia The strip of wood that covers the ends of the rafters and to which external guttering is fixed.

flashing A weatherproof junction between a roof and a wall or chimney, or between one roof and another.

frost line The depth to which the soil freezes in a given locale.

fuse box Where the main electrical service cable is connected to the house circuitry. Also the service panel.

galvanized Covered with a protective coating of zinc that prevents rust.

GFCI (ground fault circuit interrupter) A very sensitive device that quickly shuts down electrical current to prevent accidental shock.

greenfield cable The flexible steel tubing that grounds the electrical system in an older wiring scheme.

grit A number that measures the coarseness of abrasive paper, with the lower numbers (20) being very coarse, and higher numbers (180 and above) describing finer grades.

grommet A ring of rubber or plastic lining a hole to protect electrical cable from chafing.

grout A ready-mixed paste used when tiling to fill in the gaps between the tiles.

hardwood Timber cut from deciduous trees.

insulation Materials used to reduce the transmission of heat or sound. Also the nonconductive material surrounding electrical wires or connections to prevent the passage of electricity.

joist A horizontal wooden or metal beam used to support a structure like a floor or ceiling.

latex paint The most common water-based paint. Faster drying and easier to work with than oil-based (alkyd) paints but not as durable.

metal paint Either an alkyd or latex paint containing zinc or other rust inhibitors.

microporous Used to describe a finish that allows timber to dry out while protecting it from rainwater.

miter A joint formed between two pieces of wood by cutting bevels of equal angles at the ends of each piece. Also to cut such a joint.

mortise A rectangular recess cut in timber to receive a matching tongue or tenon.

nail pop The exposure of a nail head in the surface in which it is embedded, leaving a gap between the two. Often a problem with drywall installation.

nap The length of fibers on a surface, such as the fibers on a paint roller.

oxidize To form a layer of metal oxide; to rust.

pigtail wire A small length of wire connected to a longer length with a plastic connector. Often used in electrical work to ground an outlet, switch, or fixture.

pressure-treated wood Lumber that is resistant to decay and insect damage, against which it is normally guaranteed.

primer The first coat of a paint system to protect the work piece and reduce absorption of subsequent coats.

PRV (pressure relief valve) A drainage pipe designed to discharge water that has risen above its intended level in a water heater.

Romex cable Standard cable for today's wiring. Romex cable contains three wires wrapped in insulation.

scribe To copy the profile of a surface on the edge of sheet material that is to be butted against it; to mark a line with a pointed tool.

service panel The point where the main electrical service cable is connected to the house circuits. Circuit breakers protect individual circuits in the system. Sometimes called a beaker box.

sheathing The outer layer of insulation surrounding an electrical cable. Also the outer covering of a stud-framed wall that is applied beneath the wall siding.

short circuit The accidental rerouting of electricity to ground, which increases the flow of current and either blows a fuse or trips a circuit breaker.

soffit The underside of a part of a building, such as the eaves, archway, etc.

splashblock A troughlike device placed under ground pipes or downspouts that directs water away from the house.

spline roller Tool used to press window screen and spline into its frame.

stucco A thin layer of cement-based mortar applied to the exterior walls to provide a protective finish. Sometimes fine stone aggregate is embedded in the mortar. Also to apply the mortar.

stud The vertical member of a stud-framed wall.

Teflon tape Material that is wrapped around the threads of pipe fittings to prevent water and gas leaks.

template A cutout pattern to help shape something accurately.

thinner A solvent used to dilute paint or varnish.

torque A rotational force.

trap A bent section of pipe containing standing water to prevent the passage of gases; sometimes called a P-trap.

TSP (trisodium phosphate) A powerful detergent used primarily for cleaning asphalt and stone surfaces.

vinyl spline A thin strip of vinyl that anchors a window screen to its frame.

water hammer A vibration in plumbing pipework caused by fluctuating water pressure.

weather stripping A special molding fitted at the bottom of an exterior door to prevent moisture and the flow of air underneath.

Wire-Nut A common brand of plastic connector used to join electrical wire.

SOURCES

You may want to contact one of the professional associations or organizations listed below for information. They may also be helpful in answering questions you might have about standards and business practices.

American Institute of Architects
1735 New York Ave., N.W.
Washington, D.C. 20006
(202) 626-7300

American Lighting Association
435 N. Michigan Ave., Suite 1717
Chicago, Ill. 60611
(312) 644-0828

American Plywood Association
P.O. Box 11700
Tacoma, Wa. 98411
(206) 565-6600

American Society of
Interior Designers
608 Massachusetts Ave., N.E.
Washington, D.C. 20002
(202) 546-3480

Asbestos Information Association
1745 Jefferson Davis Hwy., Suite 509
Arlington, Va. 22202
(703) 979-1150

Association of Home
Appliance Manufacturers
20 N. Wacker Dr.
Chicago, Ill. 60606
(312) 984-5800

Floor Covering Installation
Contractors Association
P.O. Box 948
Dalton, Ga. 30722
(404) 226-5488

Independent Electrical
Contractors
317 S. Patrick St.
Alexandria, Va. 22314
(703) 549-7351

International Association
of Lighting Designers
30 W. 22nd St., 4th Floor
New York, N.Y. 10010
(212) 206-1281

National Association of
Home Builders
15th and M Sts., N.W.
Washington, D.C. 20005
(202) 822-0200

National Association of Plumbing,
Heating & Cooling Contractors
P.O. Box 6808
Falls Church, Va. 22040
(703) 237-8100

National Association of the
Remodeling Industry
4301 N. Fairfax Dr., Suite 310
Arlington, Va. 22203
(703) 276-7600

National Kitchen and Bath
Association
687 Willow Grove St.
Hackettstown, N.J. 07840
(908) 852-0033

INDEX

outboard posts, 89–90
outlets, electrical, 56, 162, 165–166, 171
  covers for, 6
  extension boxes for, 167–168
overspray, control of, 113–114

P

paints, painting:
  aerosol, 94, 159
  alkyd, 98, 130, 187
  alkyd primer, 130, 131
  aluminum, 112
  brushes, 184–185
  of chain-link fences, 112
  chalked, 97–98
  cleanup of, 138–139
  controlling overspray of, 113–114
  hazardous wastes and, 13
  latex, 130, 133, 142, 148, 184, 188
  latex primer, 142
  masking tape and, 86, 137
  metal, 86, 112, 188
  metal primer, 86
  oil, 148, 184
  oil primer, 142
  of paneling, 130
  removal of, 74
  of roof vents, 86
  runs, 137
  sashes, 72
  spinner tools and, 138–139
  sprayers, airless, 113
  sprayers, cup, 113
  on stucco, 105
  of textured ceilings, 148–149
  thinners, 13, 189
  of wallboard, 142–143
  over wall stains, 133–134
  water-based primer, 142
  of wood fences, 113–114
  of wrought iron, 94
paneling, 130
panels, service, 188–189
pantyhose, as filters, 18
paste wax, 19
patches, patching:
  of blacktop, 90–91
  cold, 91–92, 187
  of concrete, 87–88, 102–103
  cutting of, 128–129
  of damaged lawns, 109–110

patches, patching (cont.)
  drying of, 127
  latex base, 127
  of masonry, 87–88
  of plaster, 125–126, 127
  of stucco, 87–88
perlite, 115
pesticides, 13, 100
phosphoric acid, 36
piers, concrete, 89
pigtail wires, 8, 160, 188
pipe hangers, 153
pipe wrenches, 29, 30, 31, 32, 54, 55
planes, 181
plants, storage of, 111
plaster, patching of, 125–126, 127
pliers:
  adjustable, 17, 29, 30, 32
  locking, 183
  needle-nose, 173, 183
  slip-jaw, 183
plug covers, 6
plumber's grease, 29
plumber's oakum, 44
plumbing, 17–38
plungers, 183
plywood, 154
post holes, 89–90
pots, cooking, 6
pressure relief valves (PRVs), 33, 188
pressure-treated wood, 188
pressure washers, 84, 97, 99, 101
primers, 188
  alkyd, 130, 131
  latex, 142
  metal, 86
  oil, 142
  water-based, 142
professional associations, 191–192
propane torches, 116, 184
PRVs (pressure relief valves), 33, 188
pry bars, 182
pull-chain lamp holders, 169–170

R

radiators, 52–55
  aluminum fin, 52
  bleeding of, 52
  gravity-style, 52
  hot water, 52
  inlet valves of, 53
  steam, 53–55